For All the Family

Edited by

MICHAEL BOTTING

CPAS

KINGSWAY PUBLICATIONS
EASTBOURNE

ISBN 0 86065 314 5

Published by Kingsway Publications in association with
the Church Pastoral Aid Society (CPAS), an Evangelical
Anglican organisation set up to support and help local
parishes in their work of mission. CPAS provides materials
and training for leaders of all age groups in the church
family, including clergy, housegroup leaders and those
involved in children's and youth work.
CPAS, Athena Drive, Tachbrook Park, Warwick CV34 6NG

Produced by Bookprint Creative Services
P.O. Box 827, BN21 3YJ, England for
KINGSWAY PUBLICATIONS LTD
Lottbridge Drove, Eastbourne, E. Sussex BN23 6NT.
Printed in Great Britain

Contents

PART THREE: THE CHRISTIAN LIFE

PART FOUR: BIBLICAL CHARACTERS AND MISCELLANEOUS TALKS

Acknowledgements

One potential author that I failed to persuade to contribute any talk outlines claimed that he had never had an original thought in his life. No doubt those who have been less reticent in coming forward with talks will sympathize with these sentiments. We all know how much we are indebted to others but might not be able to recollect from where the ideas originally came.

Most, if not all of us, are especially grateful for secretarial help often freely given.

Finally I would like to thank the Bishop of Ripon for kindly writing the Foreword.

MICHAEL BOTTING

Foreword

This splendidly practical book will be of great help to those who value the teaching ministry. It will be especially useful for teaching in the context of the family. Biblical themes are presented in lively fashion with copious use of visual aids and overhead projector. The result is an attractive range of lessons which ought to capture the interest of adults and youngsters alike.

Many church members today are lacking in basic knowledge of Christian teaching. I hope that this book will help in the building up of a better-informed as well as a more profoundly faithful church.

+DAVID RIPON

Introduction

As the year of publication of *Teaching the Families* (1973, now out of print) has receded I have received an increasing number of requests for a second volume. In March 1981 the Church Pastoral Aid Society (CPAS) sought to measure the extent of the desire for a further book, and it became clear that there was a demand. Churches were asked what topics they would like to see covered in the new book, and a real attempt has been made to supply what was asked for. I sincerely pray that most of the talks will provide readers with 'meat'. Inevitably some will seem to you more like 'poison', and you will therefore need to be selective.

In the previous book I used a group of ten men known to be familiar with Family Services to provide all the talks and decide which ones should be included in the book. This time I have taken on the full editorial responsibility myself and invited contributions from a wider group of people. Because the main need was for talk outlines I have restricted the visual aid section to one item only, namely the overhead projector. It is the most serviceable piece of equipment for our purposes and can be used equally conveniently in a large cathedral or a small country church. However, in the talk outlines that follow frequent reference is made to 'Teazlegraph' with which some readers may be unfamiliar. This superlative visual aid surface was originally marketed under this name by E. J. Arnold & Sons of Leeds, but now is no longer supplied by them. This problem can easily be overcome by purchasing *nylon* velvet from any good quality fabric supplier. The material should be glued onto a sheet of plywood, say 5′ × 4′ and a dowel frame added. In order to attach anything to this board stick Velcro discs about ¼″ square onto the back of the object concerned, the number of discs depending on its size, using a strong glue like Evostik or Uhu. When the Velcro comes into contact with the nylon velvet it will adhere so well that it has been known to stay in high winds out of doors.

Alternatively the talks dependent on 'Teazlegraph' could be very easily adapted to be used with the Overhead Projector.

If further help is required on verbal or visual aids, books and sources for materials can be found in the bibliography.

As in the previous book I have included a number of talks each for Christmas, Mothering Sunday, Good Friday, Easter and Harvest.

Family services

Family Services continue to be very popular and to attract increasing congregations, though a small survey carried out by Gavin Reid of CPAS seemed to indicate that these services are often monthly rather than weekly events.

The question posed by quite a number of people in recent years has been whether the Family Service really brings people, especially fathers, into the central life of the church, or whether it is a 'safe place' for those who want to maintain only a loose tie with the church and chiefly come because it is 'lovely for the kids'.

By way of reply I would make the following points:
1. Any church service can be a safe place if people choose so to use it. All those who attend our services should be followed up pastorally in their homes. The Family Service is no magic formula or gimmick that will automatically extend the kingdom of God without tears. This means that while planning for our Family Services we need also to plan how we are going to follow up all the fringe members that Family Services undoubtedly create. In this connection I recommend either the methods advocated by Dr James Kennedy in his book *Evangelism Explosion* (see appendix) especially as adapted for the British scene by Vic Jackopson, or Michael Wooderson's approach as outlined in his Grove Booklet *Good News Down the Street* (Grove Pastoral Series No.9).

2. As has been expanded much more fully in my book *Reaching the Families* (Falcon revised edition 1976) God's basic unit is the family, and the spiritual upbringing of children is clearly the responsibility of parents, not teachers or churches (though both these can be a great help). The local church can and should help parents in their God-given task, and the whole point of a Family Service is to do just this—in two ways:

(i) by providing a 'bridge' service into the church for parents who previously have had little or no contact with Christianity;

(ii) by providing a service in which parents and children can worship together.

These services really must be designed for the whole family. David Lewis of Scripture Union told me that in many places he finds Family Services to be just Morning Prayer with a few choruses or, even worse, a kids' corner where the adults get nothing but a child's conception of God.

3. The talks at Family Services really should be proper biblical expositions, with parents as much in mind as the nine-year-olds. The visual material should be more pictorial than verbal, to keep the children's attention and teach them as much as possible. That has been the guiding principle in the outlines included in this book. However, anyone who believes he has only to copy down these outlines and make a quick visual aid is doomed to disappointment. Each talk must be prayed through and made the speaker's own by his personal illustrations. It must also be fitted to the sort of congregation he is likely to expect. On one occasion I know of, the Archbishop Lord Blanch was informed by the vicar in the vestry as he was about to preach that there were likely to be 500 scouts there. The Archbishop's comment some time later to a conference of clergy was very reasonable: 'It would have helped me in the preparation of my address if I had known a little earlier.'

A number of requests have been made for help in how to bring Family Service talks to birth, and I have opened the talks section of this book with two expanded talks and the steps that led to their existence.

The Overhead Projector

Alf was a life size cardboard cut-out and the hero of a series of talks at a boys' camp. He was very impressive when completed, but by then I had sore knees and back-ache from crouching on the floor, had spent a fortune on card, had got through a vast quantity of poster paint, and, worst of all, had managed to waste a whole day constructing him.

And then I discovered overhead projectors...

What is an overhead projector?

It is not a device for showing your holiday snaps on the ceiling.

It is not the same as an epidiascope, which projects a usually rather dull image of an opaque original (e.g. a book page) onto a screen.

It is basically a box with a glass lid in which there is a powerful projector bulb. An arm holds a small lens-and-mirror unit about 15in. above the lid. Transparent acetate sheets are placed on the lid, which is about 12in. square. The sheets are either prepared beforehand with drawings or writing, or can be written on as the projector is in use. A very bright image can be thrown onto a screen or plain wall.

What's so great about it?

(a) *Speed*. Lettering on the acetate sheets need be only slightly larger than normal handwriting, and illustrations can be only a maximum of 10in. square, so you don't waste time producing huge originals.

(b) *Colour.* Overhead projector pens normally come in black and seven bright colours: red, orange, yellow, blue, purple, brown, and green. These allow you to project a bright and colourful image onto the screen.

(c) *Large size.* With a projector of average power you can project an image of up to 8ft square. Even the most short-sighted member of your congregation should be able to see that!

(d) *Daylight use.* There is no need for black-out when you use an overhead projector. You can use it in virtually any daylight conditions other than direct sunlight on the screen.

(d) *No sticking-up problems.* As the acetate sheets are placed flat on the projector there are no problems with attaching your visual aids and no fear of their falling down. You can replace one acetate sheet with another in a second; you don't have to detach it from anything.

(f) *Use facing the congregation.* You can stand alongside the projector and face the congregation at all times. Provided the screen is set up properly beforehand there is no need for you to turn your back on your audience.

What could I use it for?

You can use it whenever and wherever you want (provided you have got a power supply!)—I have used it in children's talks, in family services, in sermons and in student conferences.

You can use it as a blackboard, jotting down suggestions shouted out by the congregation; for giving a sermon outline or summary; for colourful drawings.

I tend to use cartoons a lot—especially with a mixed-age audience. The young children love the colour and the funny faces, and the adults appreciate the humorous details. Younger teenagers, who are very wary of being spoken down to, can also laugh at the humour and feel suitably adult when they see the joke. I don't attempt life-like drawings very often, because they have to be exceptionally good to be acceptable. A sophisticated congregation, brought up on television, expect a very high standard of visual material.

In a Family Service certainly, and with adults probably, I aim to have something (preferably pictorial) on the screen at all times. I make sure that part of the picture is changed at least once every three or four minutes.

Any bright ideas?

When preparing wording use a black or bright-coloured pen. Yellow, for instance, is not bold enough to be read easily, although it is fine for blocking in a picture. Remember that young children find it difficult to read capital letters.

When preparing drawings first do an outline in black. Then turn the sheet of acetate over and colour it in on the back. It took me two years of regular use to discover this very obvious means of preventing smudging, which happens when you run a colour into a black line. (It makes your coloured pens dirty as well.)

I nearly always use a permanent ink pen as the washable ones have a nasty habit of washing off on sweaty fingers. I do have one washable pen, however, which I use when I'm experimenting with a drawing—e.g. trying to get a facial expression just right. If it's wrong I just wipe it off with a wet tissue. When I've got it how I want it, I turn the sheet over and trace the outline with a permanent pen. Then I rub off the washable original.

Incidentally, 'permanent' ink can be removed with a special plastic eraser (though not large areas of ink), with individually-packed tissues soaked in a cleaning fluid, or with a cloth and pure alcohol.

For some reason children (and adults as well, I suspect) are fascinated by a picture or diagram that is built up, but are less impressed by one that is uncovered. If you want to reveal four pictures one by one, until you have all four on the screen at once, you *could* cover the drawings with pieces of paper and then uncover them one by one, but the pieces of paper will appear on the screen as ugly black patches. Far better, once you have drawn your four pictures on an acetate sheet, to cut the sheet into four and place the pictures on the projector separately. Alternatively, if you are feeling rich (cheap acetate sheets cost about 6p each) you could do your four drawings on four sheets and then overlay them.

It is possible to make use of opaque paper. I once created a forest cut out of a sheet of paper. On the screen the trees appeared black.

Then I was able to hide cut-out acetate figures behind the trees and have them appearing to move through the forest as I moved them across the projector.

If you want high-class lettering Letraset and Mecanorma produce letter-press lettering specifically for use with overhead projectors. This is available in four or five colours. But if you are happy with black lettering, ordinary Letraset or Mecanorma letter-press is just as effective. To prevent the letters chipping I staple another piece of acetate over the top.

Another effective, though not quite so classy, method of lettering is to trace the letters from sheets of letter-press or from Letraset or Mecanorma catalogues. A coloured shadow can make the lettering even more striking.

It is possible to get photocopies printed on acetate. This way you can even project photographs, provided the original has been 'screened' (i.e. converted into dots for printing). I've seen photocopies used to project a collage of newspaper headlines.

But I can't draw!

I'm not very good at drawing either—but I can trace, and so, I expect, can you. I've built up a file of useful cartoons and drawings, and with a bit of practice it is amazing how easy it is to change a facial expression, to make somebody fatter or thinner, to give them jeans and a tee-shirt instead of a suit or first-century robes—or vice-versa. Use your imagination and indulge your sense of humour—you can get away with murder!

Anyway, if *you* can't draw, is there nobody in your congregation who can?

Strictly speaking, if you trace somebody else's work, or use it as a basis for your own drawing, you are breaching his copyright. In practice it is highly unlikely that anyone will be bothered by your making a single copy of a drawing when there is no question of financial gain. However, you might think it best to seek permission first.

What do I need?

An overhead projector capable of taking 10½ in.-square acetate sheets.

A large screen, at least 6ft square (see Appendix for suggestions about screens) or a suitable wall. If you can tilt the top of the screen towards the projector all the better—this will give sharper focusing and enable you to avoid the 'Keystone effect' (caused by projecting up at an angle, so that the bottom of the screen is nearer the projector than the top).

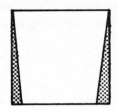

Keystone effect

A box of acetate sheets. These come in several thicknesses. The thinnest are more like cellophane and tend to warp when used with permanent pens. The thickest are very expensive. I only use them for illustrations that I know I'm going to use time and again. I normally use an intermediate thickness.

A set of pens. I would suggest:

1 or 2 washable ink pens with fine tips

A set of permanent ink pens with a medium tip

1 permanent ink pen with a fine tip

A set of 8 very broad-tipped permanent ink pens for colouring in large areas

How much and where from?

Projectors are obtainable from educational suppliers. The older ones use a very powerful bulb which requires a fan to cool it down. The bulbs for these are very expensive (about £12). The more modern projectors don't use a fan and the bulbs are much cheaper. If I was buying a projector today I would seriously consider one with two bulbs in it: you use only one bulb at a time, but if that bulb blows you can transfer to the other one at the flick of a switch.

Projector prices range from about £100 to £500. You can buy a reasonable one for about £250 + VAT.

Acetate sheets. 10½″ × 10½″ cost about £6.57 + VAT for 50, and A4 cost about £5.65 + VAT for 50.

Pens. The smaller pens cost about 24p, but specialised large ones can cost £4. Some use washable ink, others are indelible. Clearly the latter should be used only on occasions when you know you will be keeping the words or illustration indefinitely.

Acetate sheets and pens can be obtained at a good office suppliers.

JOHN ANSCOMBE
Scripture Union

PART ONE
Expanded Talks

Expanded construction

As explained in the introduction a number of enquiries have been made about how a Family Service talk comes into existence, starting much further back than the finished article shown in most of the pages that follow. In the second edition of *Reaching the Families* (pp.61–69) I give the expanded form of three talks. Here follow two more. Both were part of a series of sermons, the former on the life of David, the latter on the gifts of the Holy Spirit, so neither were especially thought to be ideal material for a Family Service. I have deliberately chosen these two talks just because they were an especial challenge.

1 David and Bathsheba

TEXT

2 Sam 11–12

AIM

After reading the passage through more than once it seemed clear that the message in a nutshell was 'Be sure your sin will find you out'. I jotted down, 'God sees sin, God hates sin, God forgives sin.'

I observed that God has not only ordained scientific laws for the well-being of his universe, but also moral laws, that cannot be flouted without serious consequences. It was not for nothing that we have been given the ten commandments.

After reading the commentaries on the passage I noted that the story has been repeated day in and day out throughout history and that there were frequent references to Psalms 32 and 51.

A story told on the media at the time was of a well-known personality who had become a Christian and who had admitted to his son he had 'fiddled' his income tax. His son had responded by admitting he regularly stole sweets from a local shop.

I became increasingly convinced that the most valuable material was the story itself, despite the length, but that it contained within it a separate story, namely Nathan's parable, which probably required a different treatment.

I considered using children or young people to do a dramatic presentation, but rejected it because of the delicate nature of the incident. But in any case the speed of the story was important if the attention was to be maintained and the message needed to be applied as the narrative moved, not simply tacked on at the end. If anyone was to tell the story it should be me, so how could I dramatise the different characters? I reduced these to three, King David, husband Uriah and prophet Nathan. (In the context of a Family Service the less said about Bathsheba the better!)

PREPARATION

I produced three different pieces of headgear to represent these three men: a crown for the king, a close fitting cap for Uriah's head and a piece of coloured weave kept on with a rope band for the prophet.

For Nathan's parable I made some black line drawings on day-glo paper similar to those in the *Good News Bible* drawn by Annie Vallotton. I stuck velcro on the back for use on my teazlegraph board.

I also put velcro on the back of two pieces of card made to look like tables of stone and on the back of the words *God* and *sin*. I cut out a red cross which could be placed across the word *sin* without making it impossible to read. I put the three words *hates, forgives, sees* in day-glo letters on teazlegraph strips to go on the teazlegraph board.

Finally I had a small table lamp to hand which could be actually switched on, and a wine bottle. I went over the story several times telling it aloud to myself till I felt more or less word perfect.

PRESENTATION

I produced the table lamp and switched it on. I then removed the bulb and asked for volunteers to come and put their fingers on the electric terminus, but got none.

'But God loves you. Would he allow the electricity to harm you?' I asked. By the nodding of heads it was clear everyone thought he would.

'What other laws has God made apart from scientific ones?'

Someone replied 'The ten commandments'.

'Yes, the moral laws'.

I put the two 'tables' on the teazlegraph board, one on each side and also *God* on the left, *sin* on the right and *hates* centred, but a little higher than *God* and *sin*.

I then told the story of David, Bathsheba and Uriah as vividly as I could wearing the crown when quoting David and the small hat when quoting Uriah. I also held the bottle when Uriah was drunk.

I then asked the congregation if they thought God knew about David's sin. They thought so and I added the word *sees* to the teazlegraph board centrally but lower than *God* and *sin*, leaving enough space between *hates* and *sees* for the third word in the middle.

I then introduced Nathan the prophet who had obviously come to know what David had done and knew he must tell him he was wrong. The problem was that as David was king he was also the judge of the people and could even judge Nathan.

I explained how Nathan eventually went to the king and told him a story, which I then told, illustrating it with the pictures from the Bible. I asked the congregation why he told that story, and soon had it explained to me. I completed the conversation between David and Nathan and added *forgives* to the teazlegraph board, explaining that God could do so because he knew Jesus would eventually die for David's sin, as he has for ours. I placed the cross across the word *sin*. I also made brief reference to parts of Psalms 51 and 32.

Finally I reminded the congregation about the father who 'fiddled' his income tax forms and the son who stole sweets. God knew and because they had confessed God forgave. I told everyone that God knew all about them and their sins, and asked them if they had confessed and whether they knew they were forgiven.

2 The Holy Spirit—pastoring and teaching

TEXT

Eph 4:7–16

AIM

When this talk was given it coincided with the arrival of two new staff members, one replacing someone who had not yet moved to his new post. This undoubtedly influenced the way the talk developed.

As already mentioned the passage seemed a difficult one for a congregation including a lot of children but I really felt it was the only one that covered the subject adequately.

On reading the text it was clear at once that Christ, through the Holy Spirit, gave gifts of pastoring and teaching to his Church, and in the parish church that included the staff, and of course the Bishop. We, in turn, were responsible for training the lay people to evangelise the world. The aim was that those who received the gospel message should be incorporated into the body of Christ, the Church. The 'cement' for the body was love.

PREPARATION

At the time I had a very talented married couple who were both artists worshipping with us. I asked if they would produce a visual aid to include a representation of Christ, cartoon faces of the Bishop and staff (I provided photographs), figures to represent Christians and people from various parts of the world. These were to be fitted into the outline of a body. The illustration on page 27 will indicate the result. I also had a dove to represent the Holy Spirit.

Two people representing the world could not be fitted into the body. They gave me an idea for the conclusion of the talk.

I had two teazlegraph boards, one on a stand and the other fixed to a horizontal beam let down from the church roof. On this the outline of the body was fixed and covered over with a black sheet. I also had two teazlegraph strips with day-glo letters on them reading *He never heard* and *He never received*.

Presentation

I told the well-known legend about the angel who asked the ascended Christ what plans he had made for spreading his gospel to the world he had just died for, and now left behind. Christ replied that he had left eleven men down on earth to spread the message.

To this the angel replied 'And what if they fail?'

To this Christ is said to have stated 'I have no other plans'.

Evangelists, pastors and teachers

I explained that the legend is not quite accurate for Christ had planned through his Spirit to provide gifts of evangelising, pastoring and teaching. I put up the visual aid representing Christ and read Eph 4:7, 8, 10 and 11. I asked who were the evangelists, pastors and teachers today and eventually received the answer that the church staff were. I added that the Bishop should be included and put up our

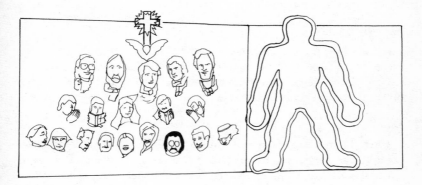

five faces. I placed the dove representing the Holy Spirit between the Christ and the staff with the beak pointing down like an arrow head.

The lay ministry

I asked 'And do we do all the work?' I quoted verse 12 and drew out from the congregation that the laity did much of it as Sunday school teachers, Bible study leaders, administrators, printers, secretaries and artists! (Here I put up 'Christian' visuals.)

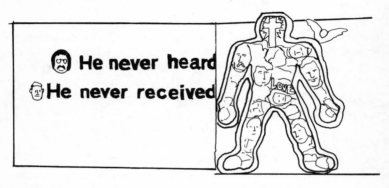

The world

I asked 'To whom do they minister?' I drew out that they were to speak to people in the world. I quoted William Temple's famous statement that the Church is the one organisation that exists for those who are not its members. (Here I put up the 'world' visuals.)

The body of Christ

I asked what was the ultimate purpose of all this and quoted again verse 12 and received the answer 'The building up of the body of Christ'. I uncovered the other teazlegraph board and transferred the pieces from the first board, leaving on it two of the 'world' figures.

Love

I referred to the gap and asked what kept the body together? Quoting verse 16 I soon received the answer, 'Love'. I quoted Bishop Dehqani-Tafti of Iran: 'Love makes us free from hate towards our persecutors.

Love brings patience, forbearance, courage, loyalty, humility, generosity, greatness of heart. Love deepens our trust in God's final victory and his eternal designs for the Church and the world.'

The two outsiders

This is what I said about the two 'world' figures:

1. *He never heard* and so is not in the body. We are responsible to go and tell the world about Christ. What part does evangelism have in our lives?

2. *He never received.* He could even be here in church this morning. If this fits you, you need to repent of your sins and receive Jesus Christ as your Saviour that you might become part of Christ's body, to serve him here on earth and one day reign with him in heaven.

MICHAEL BOTTING
Editor

PART TWO
The Christian Year

1 Advent—how Christ will return

Texts
Mt 24:43; Rev 20:15; Mt 25:14–30; Rev 5:7; 11:15; 19:16

Aim

To show what Jesus will be like when he returns.

Preparation

Obtain clothes to dress up boys. The thief will need a mask with holes
for the eyes, cloth cap, scarf, dark coat, gloves and a sack with swag in.
The judge will need a wig (can be made from cotton wool) and a
gown, the king will need a crown and a robe.

Presentation

If you use Mt 25:14–30 as the Bible reading, begin by asking what the
servant did after a long time. He came back. Explain that Jesus has
gone away and will come back. Ask for a boy to volunteer to help you
show what Jesus will be like when he returns.

Dress boy up as a thief

Ask congregation what he is. Draw out what happens when a thief
comes: he tries to take people by surprise. If there have been any thefts
in the area recently, or newspaper stories about thieves coming
unexpectedly, refer to them. Explain that Jesus will return suddenly,
unexpectedly, when people are saying 'peace' and 'security'. Point
out that Jesus is not like a thief in any other way than that he will

return when people don't expect it. People should be ready for that day by living their lives in the light.

Dress a second boy as a judge

Ask what he is. Ask what he does. He passes sentence. (Strictly speaking the jury judges but we often think of judge doing it because he 'tries the case'.) Remind people that in the creed, if you have used it, we say Jesus Christ will come as judge. What will he judge? Who will he judge? Explain first the difference between those who are Christians and those who are not. Their attitude to Jesus Christ determines it. (Refer to Rev 20:15.) Secondly, he judges Christians by what they do with their lives. Refer to Mt 25:14–30 and what the servants did. We need to live a life pleasing to Jesus.

Dress third boy as king

Explain that the Bible shows Jesus as a king. A king has a kingdom, authority and reigns. Refer to Rev 5:7; 11:15; 19:16. Draw a parallel with how we would behave if the Queen came in (stand up etc.) Point out we can pay respect to him now as we worship him.

Using the three children as visual aids, summarise points.

ALAN PUGMIRE
Manchester

2 Treasure Hunt (Bible Sunday)

TEXT

1 Pet 2:2; Ps 119:103; Jas 1:23–25; Ps 119:105

AIM

To show what the Bible is like and how it can help us.

PREPARATION

Hide objects around the church as follows. A bottle of milk in the pulpit, a jar of honey near a radiator, a mirror on the lectern, (only if eagle type), a torch below the hymn numbers. You can also attach texts to objects.

PRESENTATION

Explain that you are going to have a kind of treasure hunt. Give the clues in rhyme, and get a volunteer to look for object. If you have pew Bibles you can get people to look up verse in Bible and someone to read it out.

Clue 1

You'll find this thing that's coloured white
Up some steps to quite a height. (Milk)

Explain how milk helps baby to grow. We grow in the Christian life if we desire the Bible and drink it in. Refer to Scripture Union Bible reading.

Clue 2

Beside a thing that gives us heat
You'll find a jar that's very sweet. (Honey)

Show how honey is 'more-ish'. Bible should be like this, the more we read it, the more we should want to. The sweet things are the promises of God—over 5,000 of them, e.g. help, God's presence, Holy Spirit, guidance etc.

Clue 3

There is a bird with outstretched wings
On which you'll see unlikely things. (Mirror)

When we look in mirror we see things which need to be done. It is no good going away and forgetting. Bible shows us ourselves, we need to put right the wrong things it shows.

Clue 4

Below a list that looks like sums
Is a thing to use when winter comes. (Torch)

Show how a torch just lights up a little circle ahead of us. Bible shows us the way, as in the ten commandments, specifically at particular points in our lives when we need guidance.

Summarise points.

ALAN PUGMIRE
Manchester

3 The Bible: a library

2 Tim 3:16

Aim

To show the diversity and value of the Bible: a whole library!

Preparation

Select sixty-six books falling in the same categories as the books of the Bible, namely law (5), history (12), drama, poetry and proverbs (5), prophecy, poetry and history (17, including 12 thin ones for the minor prophets), biography/history (5), letters (21), prophecy (1). (This is well illustrated on p.57 of *The Lion Handbook to the Bible*.) Make card section-markers with simplified names—*law, history, poetry, sayings, people, letters, future*—and the number of books.

Presentation

(a) Display the library, section by section. In each section allow one or two books to be examined so that it can be seen what they are about, and place the section-marker with the section. Does anyone have a collection of books like this?

(b) Does anyone have a Bible? The Bible is just such a collection of sixty-six books!

If pew Bibles are available, turn up a reference in several of the sections to show what you mean—give the *page* number with the reference. Obvious examples would be Ex 20:12–16 (law), 1 Sam

17:49 (history), Prov 10:1, 2 (poetry), Is 7:14 (sayings), Mt 1:18 (people), 2 Cor 1:1 (letters), Rev 21:12 (future).

All these different books were written at different times by different people. Collected into one volume because they are all inspired by God and he speaks to us through them all.

(c) Mention suitable Bibles (including children's) for use by the congregation. Talk about Bible-reading notes.

(d) Conclude by reading 2 Tim 3:16.

STEVEN FOSTER
Redditch

4 Doers of the word

TEXT

Jas 1:22–27

AIM

To show that we need to *do* what the Bible says, not just read it.

PREPARATION

Obtain materials for making up your face to look very dirty. Make-up can be used, or poster-paints are harmless and easily removed. The following will also be needed: large hand-mirror, Bible, tin of sticking plaster, bank-notes (or large imitation) and a cloth for removing the make-up.

PRESENTATION

(a) Before the talk, make up your face to look dirty.

(b) Read Jas 1:22–27 and explain how the Bible tells us a great deal about God, about other people and about ourselves.

Reading the Bible is rather like looking in a mirror: you see all sorts of interesting things (look at your face in the mirror—'Oh dear! What a mess!') But some people see and then do nothing.

(c) Explain some of the things we will be doing if we read our Bibles carefully, using examples from the passage and the activities of the disciples (e.g. telling about Jesus, helping the sick, giving to the needy). In each case a child may hold up some suitable object (Bible, tin of sticking plaster, bank-note respectively) to illustrate the point.

If you choose 'bridling the tongue' (v.26) the object to be held will be provided by the child!

These things don't make a Christian, *but* if a person doesn't do them, we may suspect that Jesus makes no difference in his life (and we may be right!).

(d) Look again in the mirror. This time pretend to be really shocked at the state of your face! 'I must do something about that.' Wash off the dirt with the cloth, 'That's better!'

STEVEN FOSTER
Redditch

5 Christmas Good Newspaper

Text

Lk 2:10–11

PREPARATION

Design a sheet of cardboard to look like the front page of a newspaper. I used the title BETHLEHEM (in Roman type four inches high), followed by a red painted star, and a main heading in black: *BABY BORN IN A STABLE*. Cut out of the paper four rectangles, and place behind them in the gaps, paper in different colours with the words:

   Good News   *A Saviour*   *great joy*   *to all people*

   I then threaded nylon thread through the main card and the four rectangles I had cut out, as described in Talk 39 on page 128.

PRESENTATION

Point out that there are no newspapers on Christmas Day, but that you have brought one to make up for it, but unlike most newspapers this one is only concerned with *good news*, (move down first card). The very news that the angel brought to the shepherds at the first Christmas time (quote text).

   (a) *A message of great joy* (move down third card), quote 'Behold I bring you good tidings of great joy'. Elaborate on the joy that the coming of a baby brings. Perhaps mention that when the monarch has a son, there are 21 and 41 gun salutes in various parts of the country, a special standard is flown on Buckingham Palace, and the Navy 'splices the mainbrace' (or used to do so). When God's Son came it was a time of great joy. Christmas should therefore be a time of great joy with special events planned. But why only at Christmas? The Christmas message is always true and Christians should have the joy of Christmas in their hearts throughout the year.

(b) *A message to all people* (move down bottom card), quote verse 10. The news of a new baby in the home quickly travels. When the Queen's son was born there were news flashes on television and radio programmes were interrupted. The foreign office were informing embassies throughout the world. At the birth of God's Son the news was sent to rich and poor; to wise men by a star, shepherds by angels; to Jew and Gentile, for the shepherds would have been local Jews, and the wise men Gentiles from the East. Before Jesus ascended back to his Father in heaven, he told the disciples to 'Go tell all nations'. William Temple once said, 'If the Christian Gospel is true for anyone anywhere, it is true for everyone everywhere.' So it is a message for you: John, Mary, Uncle George, Aunt Matilda, Mummy, Daddy, Grandma. Why?

(c) *A message about a Saviour* quote verse 11, (lower second card). One of the first questions when the baby arrives is 'Is it a boy or a girl?' And then, 'What's it going to be called?'

When John Snagge announced the birth of the Queen's son he said, 'The Queen has had her baby—it's a boy.' The name was announced some time later. But when God's Son was born things were rather different. (i) Mary knew her baby was going to be a boy. (ii) The name had been given to her—Jesus means Saviour (Mt 1:21). Why was this so important? Enlarge on all people being sinners, and needing a Saviour.

(d) *Conclusion*: I wonder if you have really received the 'Good News' of Christmas? It is because we are all sinners that we need to hear the message about the Saviour. It is only those who have received the message of the Saviour who know that it is a message of great joy.

MICHAEL BOTTING
Editor

6 Three trees

TEXT

Gen 2:9; 1 Pet 2:24; Rev 22:2

AIM

To state the essentials of the Gospel by linking up three references to trees in the Bible.

PREPARATION

Draw the outline of a Christmas tree exactly symmetrically. Cut out another tree of similar shape; divide it exactly down the middle. Place second tree on top of the first and by means of sellotape or white plaster fix the tree so that the tree can be folded over to reveal three different trees, as illustrated.

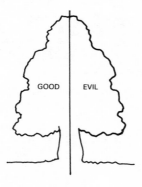

GOOD | EVIL

The first tree should look more or less like a tree but have the words *Good* and *Evil* marked on either side. The second tree should be red with a black cross painted in the middle. The third should be gold.

PRESENTATION

(a) Good and evil. Refer to Gen 2:9 and tell briefly the story of the Garden of Eden and its trees and how Adam and Eve chose evil and were turned out of the garden. How could they ever come back and resume fellowship with God.

(b) Refer to the cross (called a 'tree') and what Jesus did on it.

(c) The Tree of life. Refer back to Gen 3:22 and now to Rev 2:7 and 22:2 and speak briefly about heaven.

MICHAEL BOTTING
Editor

7 Known by God (Christmas)

TEXT

Ps 139

AIM

To show how well God knows us.

PREPARATION

Borrow the cleanest and most attractive child's doll that you can find, and gift-wrap it. Make a large (A4), colourful Christmas tag bearing the words *To Jane, love from Mummy and Daddy* and attach it to the parcel. Take two cards and write on one *They knew her* and on the other *God knows us*.

PRESENTATION

(a) Tell the following story, acting it out as you speak.

Jane is a little girl, nosey and inquisitive.

One afternoon, shortly before Christmas, Daddy at work, Mummy making mince-pies in the kitchen. Jane playing upstairs, bored, looks in parents' room; in wardrobe. Finds parcel (use your visual aid here). Pokes inside and sees what looks like hair. Seems interesting, she pulls the wrapping off a little, then in her excitement rips it off completely. How lovely it is! Then she can't re-wrap it. She panics, picks up the paper (leaving a scrap behind) and runs to the garden shed.

45

Daddy comes home. Where's Jane? She's a nosey girl, has she been in the bedroom? Scrap of paper confirms what has happened. Where is she hiding? Usually goes to the shed. Are you there Jane? What are you doing? Nothing?! Severe reprimand then back for mince-pies.

(b) Now discuss the story with the congregation, using it to show how well Jane's parents knew her. In particular:
They knew what present she wanted—they looked in their bedroom because they knew she was nosey—they knew her favourite hiding place.
At each point hold up the card *They knew her* for emphasis.

(c) Our parents know us in the same way. And God knows us even better. He knows the things which please us, hurt us, make us afraid and want to hide. (Hold up the second card in the same way—Ps 139 vv. 1–4, 7, 8 may also be read here.) God knows every part of us—and still loves us!

STEVEN FOSTER
Redditch

46

8 God with us

Mt 1:23

AIM

To show what it means for God to become man.

PREPARATION

This talk is really only suitable for the overhead projector—it would take you from Easter to Christmas to do all the illustrations large enough!

You will need to draw the following:

The words *Why is Christmas like this?*

A schoolmaster (in front of a blackboard).

The same schoolmaster sitting at a desk with the pupils.

A traditional Christmas stable scene.

A baker.

The same baker queuing outside a bread shop.

An architect—looking at plans.

The same architect sleeping rough.

An artist painting.

The same artist painting by numbers.

The words *Emmanuel—God with us*.

Jesus as an adult, looking tired.

Jesus on the cross.

PRESENTATION

Put on the screen the words *Why is Christmas like this?* without explanation. Tell the congregation you're going to introduce them to four people. As they look at each of them and what they're doing you want them to think, 'Why is Christmas like this?' (Clear the screen.)

Mr Chips (Show the picture of the schoolmaster.) What do you think his job is?... But he gave up being a teacher, and what do you think he did? (They won't have a clue.) (Remove the picture and replace it with one of the schoolmaster sitting with the pupils.) He came to school as a pupil! (Add the words *Why is Christmas like this?* and immediately add the picture of the stable scene. Clear the screen.)

Mr Bunn (Show the picture of the baker.) What do you think his job is?... Every day after he'd finished baking he'd come home for breakfast, and then what do you think he did? (Remove the picture and replace it with the one of the baker in the queue.) He joined the queue at the bread shop! (Add the words *Why is Christmas like this?* and immediately add the picture of the stable scene. Clear the screen.)

Mr Wren (Show the picture of the architect.) What do you think his job is?... What sort of house do you think he lived in? A fantastic one! (Remove the picture and replace it with the one of him sleeping rough. Add the words *Why is Christmas etc.*, and the stable scene as before. Clear the screen.)

Mr Von Gaff (Show the picture of the artist.) What do you think he does for a living?... He painted hundreds of beautiful pictures that sold for thousands of pounds. Then he took up a different sort of painting. (Remove the picture and replace it with the one of the artist painting by numbers.) He did painting by numbers! (Add the words *Why... etc.* and the stable scene as before. Clear the screen.)

Jesus Refer back to the reading which will have included Mt 1:23. Can you remember what name it gave to Jesus (Put the words *Emmanuel—God with us* at the top of the screen.)

When Jesus was born it was God coming to live with us. It was crazy—like Messrs Wren and Bunn. Jesus gave up being with his Father and having angels around him for a smelly stable (show the stable scene again). He knew what it was to be tired (add picture of Jesus looking tired, hated, misunderstood). He knew what it was to

48

die (add picture of Jesus on the cross)—for us. If he'd stayed in heaven he would never had to do those things. But he gave up heaven because he loved us. Because he did that it meant he could know what it's like to be a man, he could teach us what God is like and what he wants, and he could die for us so that we could be forgiven.

Jesus being born as a baby was God coming to live with us—which is what *Emmanuel* means.

JOHN ANSCOMBE
Scripture Union

9 What Jesus faced (Christmas)

TEXT
Mt 2; Jn 1:10–12

AIM

To consider what happened to Jesus soon after his birth, and the reactions to Jesus today.

PREPARATION

Draw on five acetate sheets, so that they can be taped to an OHP transparency mount, and overlapped (one at a time) to form the words *Manger*, *Danger* and *stranger*—the base sheet simply having the word *anger* on it.

(N.B. The drawings can be taken out of *Help, I can't draw!* see appendix).

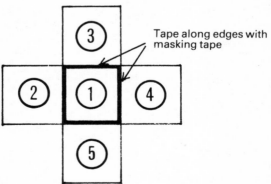

PRESENTATION

(Begin with sheet 2 overlapping sheet 1)

50

Manger

This is the centre of our thoughts today—the manger at Bethlehem.

> *Lo within a manger lies*
> *He who built the starry skies*

(Emphasise the wonder of it—not only that Jesus came to earth, but that he chose to be born in a dirty, smelly stable.) Surely, though, everyone is going to welcome him? (Speak about the joy of the shepherds, and some time later on, the worship of the wise men.) But not everyone was happy with the news.

(Replace sheet 2 with sheet 3)

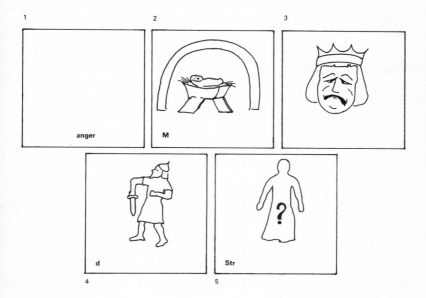

Anger

Who might this be? (King Herod) When the wise men came to him—and even more so when they failed to return (Mt 2:16), he was furious. This was very much in keeping with his character—during his life, he murdered his wife, mother-in-law and three sons. The

Emperor Augustus said once that it was 'safer to be Herod's pig than Herod's son'.

Why was he so angry now? No doubt because of his jealousy at someone else being called 'King of the Jews'. He wanted to rule himself, and not to give allegiance to anyone else. Although we may not be like Herod, who really rules in our life as king—self or Christ?

With Herod, it didn't just stop at anger.

(Replace sheet 3 with sheet 4)

Danger

Herod was so furious that he ordered the massacre of all the infant boys in Bethlehem (Mt 2:16b)—*All the little boys he killed, at Bethlehem in his fury.* (Emphasise the danger to Jesus—the dream of Joseph—the flight into Egypt—Mt 2:13–15.) Jesus was now a refugee—and Christmas is often an appropriate time to remember people in this situation today. However, he was alive—it was not God's plan that Jesus should die as a baby. Some 30 years later, though, this same Jesus was *not* rescued from danger and death—he deliberately went to death on the cross for us (Phil 2:8 and the prophecy in Is 53:5). What is our attitude to Jesus?

(Replace sheet 4 with sheet 5)

Stranger

Herod was amongst the first of many people who rejected the claims of Christ—to them he was a stranger. (Perhaps link with the carol: *Child in the manger, infant of Mary, outcast and stranger...*) John writes: 'He was in the world, and the world was made through him, yet the world knew him not' (Jn 1:10). The message of Jesus is being spread throughout the world over this Christmas, and in this town, and in this church. Jesus is making himself known—but is he a stranger to you?

Close with the message of Jn 1:12, and, possibly:

> *O come to my heart, Lord Jesus*
> *There is room in my heart for Thee*

PETER BANNISTER
Bridgwater

10 A Christmas talk— based on the Rubik cube

AIM

To show that Christmas is but one side of the real meaning of Christianity.

PREPARATION

Obtain these materials:

(a) One square wooden tea-chest, as used by removal firms. (This may need selecting carefully, as many such packing cases are noticeably oblong.) Local firms are likely to be willing to lend, or donate such a tea-chest.

(b) Fluorescent card in six different colours.

(c) Black Velcro strip (both hook and fuzzy sides).

(d) Glue.

(e) Black vinyl sticky tape.

° Cover the six sides of the tea-chest with the coloured card (the lid opening may need to be sealed with a panel of firm cardboard first).

° Rule up thick black lines to simulate cube sections with a broad felt pen. Alternatively, the black sticky vinyl tape does the job more neatly and also secures the coloured panels.

° Prepare matching card panels, in identical colours; cut these into squares, and paste on 4 inch lettering (in black or white, as stands out best) to make up the six key words of the talk (see below).

° Glue small squares of the *fuzzy* half of velcro strip on to the tea-chest panels, at the corners of each individual square. (These will be invisible if the dividing black lines are thick enough.)

° Glue small squares of the *hook* half of velcro strip on to the reverse corners of each of the individual matching coloured square panels, on which the lettering has been placed.

PRESENTATION

Get several competent children to come out and give a high-speed demonstration of cube-solving. Provide suitable patter about baffled adults taking two hours to do one side of the cube—while children can conquer the thing in under a minute. Then produce giant cube and place on appropriate stand.

Stage 1

(a) Let's see if we can, between us, solve the cube. We'll try the first side. (Put up 'B' and guide through till *Bethlehem* is guessed. Complete first side.)

(b) A person would surely be regarded as rather foolish if they claimed to have mastered the cube—when they really had only done one or two sides? Everyone could see they had only got a small part of it right so far.

Yet lots of people do this with Christianity. It is always good to see many people at church in December—but sad if they don't go on to grasp the full meanng of Bethlehem.

(c) Now let's do the second side. (Put up two or three letters of *Christmas* and let children complete the word. Apply meaning of nativity: the beginning.)

(d) Words so far: *BETHLEHEM*

CHRISTMAS a third of the cube is done.

Stage 2

(e) Have you ever had someone point out to you, at night, the twinkling lights of a jet plane, far above? Often you can't find it because it has moved on from the place originally spotted.

So it is also with Jesus. He was born at Bethlehem in a stable. It is right that we celebrate Christmas. But not that we stop there. He didn't stay a child any more than we do. He moved on. And he always knew where he was headed for. Do you know?

(f) Let's see if we can do sides three and four of this cube. Help children by providing a few letters, to complete the next two sides, bearing the words:

JERUSALEM
CRUCIFIED

(g) Apply appropriately the meaning of Christ's death for each of us at Easter.

Stage 3

(h) Still there remain two sides to be done. So also, many people understand the meaning of Christmas and Easter, but fail to move on from there to understand and fulfil the final aspects of God's purpose in sending Jesus to be the Saviour of the world. Let's try and understand this as we finish this giant cube.

(i) Briefly relate (or draw from the children) the post-Easter events of Ascension, Pentecost and the birth and task of the Christian church.

(j) As you do so, complete sides five and six:

PENTECOST
DISCIPLES

(k) Apply the implication of God's purpose through the gift of the Spirit for our service as well as our salvation.

Conclusion

At first sight, a jumbled-up Rubik cube can be a most daunting prospect. But the encouraging thing is, that, although difficult, it *can* be restored from any tangle, or angle.

So it is also with our lives. There is no individual, or church situation, that God is not able to put to rights, from any degree of confusion. 'He can save to the uttermost'.

It all depends on our grasping the fullness of his purpose in Christ. Response is needed to Christmas, Easter and Whitsun.

This means being committed, both to him and his people, the church. Believing equals belonging.

Many people have managed a few sides of a cube—and then lost their way and lost heart. Faith is needed to press on when 'almost there' to complete all the remaining sides.

Settle for nothing less in your response to all God has done for you in Jesus Christ. Do not be a one-sided Christian. Resolve to go all the way with him, and for him.

JOHN SIMONS
Nailsea, Avon

11 The Murder of the Innocents

TEXT

Mt 2:13–23

AIM

To show how God dealt with the cruelty and sadness of the world.

PREPARATION

Use double-sided board or large board with the two presentations in parallel, one side representing heaven and the other earth. The words are filled in using ladder lettering.

Heaven (use stiff yellow paper or card).

° Central disk and eight strips radiating from it, four of these laddered for words.

° Symbols representing: peace

joy   singing

love

Earth (use stiff green paper or card).

° Central disk representing the world.
° Three yellow strips.
° Five green strips laddered for words.
° Symbols on yellow card representing:

Mary and Joseph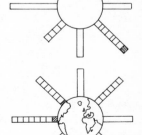

57

shepherds

Wise men

° Symbols on green card representing: anger

danger fear

murder sadness

° Symbols in red card representing:

manger grown man cross †

PRESENTATION

Introduction

If this is just after Christmas, discuss what makes Christmas a good or sad occasion.

Heaven

Before Jesus was born in Bethlehem, he lived in a wonderful place where there was no sadness or things that spoil our lives. God was there and all the good things of life. (Uncover the visual aid representing heaven but without words filled in or symbols.) Explain that heaven is a place of joy, peace, singing and love, and as you do so fill in the letters and add the symbols beside the words.

God wanted everyone to enjoy heaven with him, but saw the sadness in the world and that people were not good enough to be in heaven, so he thought of a plan.

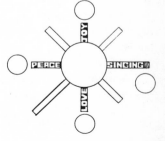

Earth

(Uncover the other visual aid representing Earth without words or symbols).

Jesus came to earth as a baby (fix the

manger in centre of 'world'). Some people were kind to him. (Explain as you add symbols of Mary and Joseph, shepherds, and wise men beside yellow strips.)

But this world could also be a sad place as the king was cruel and jealous. Tell the story (as you add the words and symbols to show *anger—danger—fear—murder—sadness*).

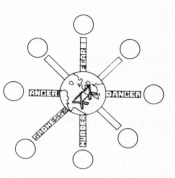

God's reaction

He was pleased that some people welcomed Jesus, not surprised, though saddened at the suffering caused. But God didn't take Jesus away. Jesus grew to be a man (replace manger with figure of grown man).

He is Emmanuel—God with us.

He is Jesus—Saviour (replace man with cross).

He died to defeat Satan and all the sad things Satan causes. Those who trust Jesus will one day go to heaven where there is no more sadness. (Refer to first visual aid.)

JUDITH ROSE
Bradford

12 The gifts of the wise men
(Suitable for a Brownie Thinking Day or Toy Service)

TEXT
Mt 2:11

AIM
To explain the significance of the wise men's gifts.

PREPARATION
Can be told without visual aids, but can be very effective based round an enlarged Christmas stocking or Christmas cracker. Gifts with the words *gold* marked on them are produced out of the stocking or cracker. If the cracker idea (or even three crackers) is used, the bang can be made with a toy gun that fires caps. This also ensures the congregation is kept alert!

PRESENTATION
Enquire if any members of the congregation will be hanging up stockings at Christmas. Recap the story of the wise men bringing presents to the baby Jesus.

(a) *Meaningful gifts*
If someone received a lot of soap for Christmas they might say, 'Is someone trying to tell me something?' All the wise men's gifts tell us something important about Jesus. Enlarge on each:
- ° Gold—Tribute for a King
- ° Frankincense—Worship for God
- ° Myrrh—Balm for one who died

(b) *Wonderful gifts*

Explain that these gifts were very costly, quite apart from all the time and trouble taken to get them to their destination. Tell a story of a child that brought a broken toy to a Toy Service; it had not cost much. Express the hope that no broken toy was given at the service today.

The wise men brought such costly gifts because of who Jesus was. The greatest gift we can give Jesus is our lives, and he especially wants us while we are young. Refer to D. L. Moody's observation that twelve and a half lives were given to Christ at one of his meetings, i.e. twelve children and one adult.

(c) *Useful gifts*

Explain that we would not expect our fathers to be given handbags for Christmas, or our mothers razors. The wise men's gifts were very useful for the Holy Family's trip to Egypt: gold to use as money, frankincense to keep away flies and make the home smell nice, myrrh would be excellent baby powder. If we want our lives to be really useful we must put them into the hands of Jesus.

Perhaps end with the story of Victor Trumper, the cricketer who once scored a century with a child's bat. The secret was that the little bat was in the hands of the master player.

MICHAEL BOTTING
Editor

13 The creation of man

TEXT

Gen 2:4–25

AIM

To think about man's creation without taking sides on the evolution issue.

PREPARATION

Have the seven headings below on teazlegraph strips ready to place on a teazlegraph board, and also a picture of an ape. Surreptitiously have a man under a blanket, near where you give the talk. Also have a piece of coal, chalk, cellar of salt, glass of water, portable musical instrument, a painting and a garden fork. Ask the organist to be ready to play the opening bars of some stirring music. Have a sign-post with right and wrong on it.

PRESENTATION

Ask in what section of a library the congregation would expect to find the Bible or books about it, Religion or Science? Explain that religion is for all time and must be explained so that the simplest of people can understand it. It explains, or should do, the purpose of man in the world. Science, on the other hand, attempts to explain *how* the world works. Today as we think about our creation, we are not going to say if our first parents looked like this (show picture of an ape), but see what the Bible says about what sort of creation God made man to be. God gave man:

(a) *Body* (v.7a) dust from the ground. Produce the coal, chalk, salt and water and explain that that is what we are chiefly made of, costing about a pound. *Adam* is the Hebrew word for ground from which man came and gets his name. Reveal the lifeless man lying on the ground, and explain that a lifeless body is no use, but only fit to be put back into the ground—'dust to dust'.

(b) *Life* (v.7b) 'God...breathed into his nostrils the breath of life and man became a living being.' The man on the ground 'comes to life'.

(c) *Home* (vv.8–9 quote or explain). Eden means a place of delight with its plants and fruit. Earth is home—even for astronauts!

Explain that everything that has been considered so far would be true of animals. They need, and God has given them, bodies, life and home. However God has given man, but not animals:

(d) *Choice* (vv.9, 16–17 quote). Reveal sign-post and get the man to look at it and seem puzzled. Explain that this is the reason why the Bible says that man has been made in the image of God. He is a moral being who can choose between right and wrong.

(e) *Culture* (vv.9–14 quote or summarise). Speak about the beauty in the garden. Man has been made to enjoy art (show picture), music (pick up musical instrument and ask organist to play at this point). Perhaps explain that our dogs are not interested in the TV unless a dog barks.

(f) *Work* (v.15 quote). Reveal garden fork and explain that God has a special purpose for man. Man is happiest when engaged in satisfying work, which is why it is so tragic when so much modern industrial work is so boring and so many people cannot get work at all. Work was purposeful and pleasant in Eden and will be in heaven.

(g) *Wife* (v.18 quote). Man is essentially a social creature, but found no real companion amongst the animals. Just as Adam was *specially* made, so was Eve *specially* made for him, not to be his slave, but his queen.

That is what God originally gave man, but Christians know God gave us much more. Enlarge on John 3:16 briefly.

MICHAEL BOTTING
Editor

14 A talk for Tear Fund Sunday

Text
Jn 6:1–14

Aim

Stimulate concern and generosity for the Third World and for helping charitable organisations like TEAR Fund.

Preparation

Obtain the assistance of a church family and the equipment named in the presentation. Perhaps have an OHP or teazlegraph board for the main headings of the talk and the sub-headings under 'Secret of the child' (below).

Presentation

Introduce the talk by mentioning picnics (with special reference to any church picnics you may have, where the crowd may be quite large). Refer to what must have been one of the largest picnics in history and describe the feeding of the 5,000—which may only have been the number of men.

(a) *Size of the crowd* Consider the problem of feeding such a large number following Jesus' discussion with Philip. Mention the very much greater problem of feeding about 2,000 million very hungry people in the world today. But it is not just food they need. Let's take a typical western family.

(The pre-arranged family come and sit on comfortable chairs in front of the congregation. Nearby are tables carrying the various items to be taken away from them.)

Food: take away tinned food and cake. Leave some potatoes and beans.

Clothing: take away all outer clothing. Leave shoes on the man only.

Home: remove door (made of cardboard), chairs, tables and TV. Leave a blanket.

Schooling: remove all books.

Public services: remove telephone (borrowed from Telecom), bottles of medicine. Leave a very old bicycle.

Money: allow £2.

Ask the congregation what to do. Do we send them away? Jesus said to his disciples 'You give them something to eat' (NIV).

(b) *Smallness of the contribution* (Refer to v.9). Explain the barley loaves would be poor man's food and fish probably no more than a pickled relish. The lad would only be a small boy who would not carry much. Then describe what Jesus did and the enormous supply of food there was, as implied in vv.11–13.

Go on to explain that compared to the needs of the world we ourselves have little to offer, like the lad, but as St Augustine put it, 'Without God we cannot, without us God will not.'

(c) *Secret of the child*

° *He gave his small contribution to JESUS*—that was all, but little becomes much when God is involved. Supremely God wants, not our money, but us.

° *He gave ALL his contribution to Jesus*—he held nothing back. Refer to the widow's mite and the story of Ananias and Sapphira. God knows how much we give and how much we withhold. He does not ask of us more than he was prepared to give. He so loved that he gave Jesus.

° *He did not go without HIMSELF*—all were filled, which must have included the lad. Whether it be our money, possessions or our whole lives we shall never lose by giving to God's work, but rather lose if we do not give. End with a suitable story or mention the testimony of tithers, who, once they start, never give the practice up.

MICHAEL BOTTING
Editor

15 Mary (Mothering Sunday)

TEXT

Lk 1 and 2

AIM

To show Mary's responsibility as a mother—and compare with mothers today.

PREPARATION

- ° Four cards for teazlegraph board: *Her service*
  Her sense
  Her sorrow
  Her Saviour
- ° Large drawing of Mary
- ° Large cross, sufficient to cover Mary.

PRESENTATION

(Put up drawing of Mary in centre of board.)

Mary had a special responsibility as the mother of Jesus—but there were certain things about her which are true of all the best of mothers.

(a) *Her service* (put up on board)

Not a popular word today!

Lk 1:38 'I am the handmaid of the Lord' or (GNB) 'I am the Lord's servant'. It was not easy for her!

Think of the ways in which mothers serve us.

(b) *Her sense* (put up on the board)

Mothers are so often full of common-sense! Mary had that—and more! (Lk 2:19 'But Mary kept all these things, pondering them in her heart.' And Lk 2:51). She couldn't understand everything—but she did have the sense to consider Christ and the amazing things that happened. Have we the sense to consider Christ in this way?

(c) *Her sorrow* (put up on board)

Some of the deepest problems and worries that mothers have come over their children. There would be something wrong if this wasn't the case. Lk 2:35—Simeon's words to Mary—'and a sword will pierce through your own soul also'. Mary was to have many sorrows in her life, as she saw her son rejected—in one sense, the whole of her life, up to the crucifixion, was lived in the shadow of the cross. (Place the cross on the board, over Mary.)

(d) *Her Saviour* (put up on board)

Mary was a wonderful and remarkable woman—but she needed a Saviour. (Lk 1:46–47 Mary's words: 'My soul magnifies the Lord, and my spirit rejoices in God my Saviour.')

Later in her life, after the crucifixion and resurrection, we find Mary meeting together with the disciples to pray in the upper room (Acts 1:14).

If a 'good' person like Mary needed a Saviour, the same is true of us, whether we think we are 'good' mothers, fathers, sons or daughters. Do you know Jesus as your Saviour?

PETER BANNISTER
Bridgwater

16 The family of God in the letter to the Ephesians

(Suitable for Mothering Sunday)

TEXT

The letter to the Ephesians

AIM

To draw out the teaching on the Christian family found in Paul's letter to the Ephesians.

PREPARATION

Prepare for the teazlegraph board open hands (to represent God the Father), a family of father, mother, boy, girl and baby that would be typical of the church congregation, a large card with the word *sin* on it, a large red cross to go across the word *sin* without totally covering it, a small figure of a church building and a dove to represent the Holy Spirit. Notes for this talk could be on a scroll.

PRESENTATION

Most of us like receiving letters, even though some turn out to be bills or bad news. We are going to look at one bringing good news, written by Paul to a number of churches, especially Ephesus. He seemed to have a lot to say about families, including the family of God.

The Fatherhood of God

Refer to 3:14–15 and point out that families are God's bright idea. (Put up hands at top of teazlegraph board.) To know what it is to be a real father we have to look at God, the Father. God in his great love wanted more and more people to love, so he created man to be a husband and father, and woman to be a companion, wife and mother. (Put man and woman up on left and right of board with space for *sin* to go between them. Preferably have them looking away from each other.) God commanded them to have children (Gen 1:28). (Put up children at bottom centre of board.)

Sin

Refer to the family all being so far apart and mention the Fall and the break up of the family, perhaps with reference to Adam, Eve, Cain and Abel. Between us and God, man and woman, parents and children is *sin*. (Put word in the centre of board.) Perhaps quote Eph 2:3. Unless something is done at home level there is trouble. A great educationalist has said 'The character of your children is being determined in your homes.' Very many young men of 25–35 are in prison today. Often a common feature about them is that they come from divided homes.

The peace of Christ

The purpose of his coming was to bring peace (2:14–16). To put this simply (putting up the cross over *sin*) he died for our sins, bringing us in touch with God and one another. (If the board has been properly laid out the hands of God, the man, the woman and the children should be at the extremities of the cross.) The congregation might be challenged at this point about their relationship with Jesus, referring to 2:8–9, and being told the way to find peace with God.

The church (2:19)

Once you have accepted Christ as Saviour, you become members of God's household, the family of God, the Church, (put up church). Explain that the real meaning of Church is not the building but the people who use it for worship and fellowship. God has given to the Church pastors and teachers (4:11) to help us understand the Bible and how we ought to live the Christian life, which includes family life. They do not take over the upbringing of children, but help parents in the Christian upbringing of their children.

Family relationships

Comment on (a) wives to husbands (5:21–24); (b) husbands to wives (5:25–33) if you had the man and woman facing away from each other on the board, reverse them to face one another now; (c) children to parents (6:1–3); (d) parents to children (6:4). How can we possibly live up to such a standard?

The Spirit (put up dove on board)

Refer to 2:22 and 5:18. We cannot expect to live this life without the power of the Spirit of Jesus within us. Explain that when Paul wrote in 3:17 about Christ dwelling in our hearts, the real meaning is that he should 'feel at home' there. If he is in each member of our families, then indeed ours will be a very happy family, which is what God, 'the Father, from whom every family in heaven and on earth is named' desires for us all.

MICHAEL BOTTING
Editor

17 Palm Sunday

AIM

To bring the events of the first Palm Sunday vividly to life.

PREPARATION

As all of your congregation will be taking part in this dramatic reading you will need to supply plenty of copies. You will also need two people to play the parts of Abel and Benaiah (the Pharisees). Paper streamers are good fun as an optional extra.

PRESENTATION

The time: Palm Sunday, about AD 30.

The place: Jerusalem, Israel.

ABEL: *(a Pharisee):* What enormous crowds there are this year for the Passover holiday!

BENAIAH: *(another Pharisee):* Yes, the shops are absolutely packed. Look over there, Abel, what is it?

CROWD 1:   A man, coming down the Mount of Olives, towards Jerusalem.

CROWD 2:   He's riding on...a donkey! Who is it?

CROWD 1:   It's Jesus. It's Jesus the Prophet! He comes from Nazareth.

CROWD 2:   Jesus?

CROWD 1:   Yes! He's the one who raised Lazarus (b) from the dead. Look at the people round him. They're throwing their cloaks down in front on him.

CROWD 2:   Under the donkey's feet!

ALL: *(loudly):* Come on, let's join in!

CROWD 2:   Let's cut down leaves from the palm (a) trees!

ALL: (c) Chop, chop, chop, chop. He's nearly here.

CROWD 1:   Praise to David's Son!

CROWD 2:   God bless him who comes in the name of the Lord!

CROWD 1:   Here he comes now.

ALL: (d) Clip clop, clip clop, CLIP CLOP!

CROWD 1:   Praise God!

CROWD 2:   God bless him who comes in the name of the Lord!

CROWD 1:   God bless (e) THE KING who comes in the name of the Lord!

ALL: *(waving palms):* (f) God bless the King of Israel.

ABEL: This is terrible. The whole world is following him.

BENAIAH: I remember a prophet once wrote about this:
             Shout for joy you people of Jerusalem!
             Here comes your king, riding on a donkey!

CROWD 2:   Praise God! Hosanna Lord!

ABEL: Can't you all shut up?

CROWD 1:   No, if we did, the stones of the buildings would shout instead.

CROWD 2:   Look, he's going into the Temple. Perhaps it's his (g) coronation.

ALL: Praise God!

CROWD 1:   Peace in Heaven and glory to God!

CROWD 2:   Praise to David's Son!

ALL: *(waving palms and throwing streamers).* (h) Praise God!
             Hosanna Lord! Hosanna! Hosanna! Hosanna!!
             (break into song, 'Sing Hosanna!')

Set the scene and explain why today is called 'Palm Sunday' (refer to (a) in text).

Introduce the two Pharisees and divide the congregation into Crowd 1 and Crowd 2. (If they are unevenly split, Crowd 1 should be the larger.)

Distribute the streamers (if available) and explain how and *when* to throw them.

Rehearse the reading, to teach the idea of reading together and coming in loudly on each cue.

Go through the text, picking out points needing special explanation or rehearsal. In particular note:

(b) the reference to Lazarus—partly explaining Jesus' popularity.

(c) the sound of chopping can be imitated by clapping in time.

(d) feet are inevitable here!

(e and g) see what the people were thinking.

(f) we might wave banners today. Instead we'll wave the palms of our hands!

(h) this should be a tremendous climax—save the streamers for this.

Now do your reading. If you lead the crowd parts firmly and enthusiastically from the front they will join in easily.

End with a short talk explaining what did actually happen afterwards...to Jesus *and* the crowd. The change of mood is very effective.

STEVEN FOSTER
Redditch

18 Not good enough (Good Friday)

TEXT

Amos 7:7–9; Dan 5:27; Rom 3:23; Jn 14:6

AIM

To show that we are not good enough by God's standards.

PREPARATION

Obtain or make a plumbline (a weight on a piece of string will do), a set of weighing scales, preferably of the balance kind, and a measure, such as is used by workmen. Some flour or other kitchen commodity and a piece of wood under two feet long would also be useful. A spirit level can also be used.

PRESENTATION

Begin by going as high as you can (pulpit steps or ladder—show plumbline). Ask what it is used for. It shows when a wall is not straight. (Show spirit level if being used.) It indicates when something is not straight.

Refer to Amos 7:7 and how God was going to test his people to see if they were straight or true. God puts a plumbline on us—the law—to show us how he expects us to live. But we are not straight; we are not the kind of people he wants us to be.

(Produce weighing scales. Get a girl to weigh out an amount of flour, but have insufficient flour for that amount.) Try to draw out of her that she has not enough. Refer to the story of Belshazzar's feast and the writing on the wall (Dan 5:27) showing he was too light. Explain again that however good we are, it is not enough for God.

Tell audience you want a piece of wood two feet long for a job that has to be done. (Produce wood. Get a boy to measure it and find it is too short.) Read out Rom 3:23. We don't reach God's standards. Only Jesus is true (Jn 14:6), perfect and reached God's standard.

> *There was no other good enough*
> *To pay the price of sin,*
> *He only could unlock the gate*
> *Of heaven and let us in.*

ALAN PUGMIRE
Manchester

19 The people for whom Christ died (Good Friday)

TEXT

Rom 5:6–11

AIM

To show the kind of people for whom Christ died.

PREPARATION

Obtain a bottle of water from the dirtiest local river or canal. Label it 'Pure... (name of canal)'. Have a glass of water from the tap, a bottle of poison (so labelled) preferably which changes the colour of water—weed killer might do. (Alternatively something less dangerous—the main thing is that it change the colour of the water.) An old plate, broken in two, and a pair of shoelaces are also needed.

PRESENTATION

Ask if anyone is thirsty. Say you have some special water (produce your 'Pure...'). Is anyone willing to drink it? Refer to Rom 5:6–11 especially v.8. Point out the water you have is natural water which has not been through any purifying process, therefore it is unfit to drink. The people for whom Jesus died are naturally unfit for God. Refer to Is 64:6. Although water may be 'Pure...' it is filthy. (Produce glass of water and see if anyone is prepared to drink from it. If not then do so yourself. Then add poison.) Point out it is only a very little drop and see if anyone is prepared to drink! Some people say they are not very bad. It doesn't matter whether we are very bad or not very bad, we are all *sinners*—the impure people for whom Jesus died.

Refer to verse 10 and show we were *enemies*. We have a broken relationship (show broken plate). Explain God and man are apart. Refer to Col 1:21. Point out that you can try to mend plate, but it will never be the same again. Say that people try to mend their broken relationship with God by being nice or religious. We cannot mend it that way. We are enemies.

(Show shoelaces.) Remind them that they cannot pick themselves up by own shoelaces. Try it! Point to v.6 to show that we are *helpless* to do anything about our condition. Illustrate from someone in bed very ill. Some people try to help themselves but God says we can't. Refer to Eph 2:8–9.

Summarise that we are sinners, enemies, helpless and point out Christ died to make us clean, to make us God's friends and to lift us up. End with an evangelistic prayer in which we admit we are sinners, enemies and helpless.

ALAN PUGMIRE
Manchester

20 Who crucified Jesus? (Good Friday)

TEXT

Acts 2:23

AIM

To teach that Christ died for *our* sins. The talk uses a somewhat startling audio-visual aid.

PREPARATION

With the aid of a fret-saw cut out the shape of a large hand in plywood and paint it pink. Prepare seven small thin cards with the following words printed in black on each side respectively:

Peter	*Pride*
Judas	*Greed*
Jews	*Hate*
Witnesses	*Lying*
Herod	*Lust*
Pilate	*Selfishness*

The last card should have *God* on one side and *Love* on the other in red. Have a hammer and seven large nails available.

PRESENTATION

Begin the talk by asking the question, 'Who crucified Jesus Christ?' Agree that of course it was the soldiers, but that was only because it was their duty. Really they were the least to blame. There are two other answers.

First you and I did. But you say, 'Not me. I would never have done that'. That is what Peter said. But Peter crucified Jesus by his pride. (Produce the card with *Peter* on one side and *Pride* on the other).

Peter boasted he would never deny Jesus and then denied him only a few hours later. Have you ever been proud? You and I crucify Jesus Christ by pride, (nail *Pride* to the hand).

In the same way enlarge on *Judas, Jews, Witnesses, Herod* and *Pilate*. (Nail these to the hand also.) You and I crucified Jesus Christ. What are we doing about it? There is nothing we can do about it.

Someone else crucified Jesus Christ: God! God sent his Son into the world to die for us. Jesus said, 'No man taketh my life from me.' Later he said, 'Not my will but thine be done.' To Pilate he said, 'You would have no power over me unless it had been given you from above.' God sent Jesus to the cross because he loves us. (Show the card with *God* on one side and *Love* on the other side and nail it to the other side of the hand.)

So Jesus died because of our sins and for our sins. If you find this message astonishing then listen to the words of Peter in his first sermon on the day of Pentecost. Quote Acts 2:23 slowly. End by exhorting the congregation to receive Jesus as Saviour.

MICHAEL BOTTING
Editor

21 The faces of Barabbas (Passion Sunday, Good Friday, etc.)

TEXT
Lk 23:18–19, 25

AIM

To see how the crucifixion affected Barabbas—and us.

PREPARATION

Draw five faces, depicting different emotions, on card or acetate sheets (for OHP).

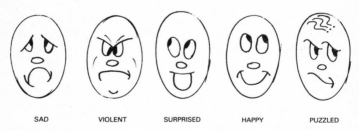

SAD   VIOLENT   SURPRISED   HAPPY   PUZZLED

PRESENTATION

You can often tell how a person feels by the look on his face. The man we are going to think about had every reason to look like this:

(Produce SAD face)

He was in a prison cell which was probably cold, damp and depressing. Worse than all that, he was under sentence of death, and by crucifixion. Why?

(Produce VIOLENT face)

His name was Barabbas, and the Bible describes him as a robber (Jn 18:40), a rebel and a murderer (Lk 23:19)—a man of violence.

Imagine it is early in the day. There comes the sound of heavy footsteps and the rattle of keys. They have come to take him and put him to death. The cell door opens, and he hears the rough voice of the prison guard: 'Get up, Barabbas....

(Produce SURPRISED face)

...you're free'. He can hardly believe it. Off he goes, as quick as he can, before they change their minds!

(Produce HAPPY face)

He expected to be killed—and now he is free! Imagine his joy! I wonder what happened next? Perhaps this may have been the next expression on his face:

(Produce PUZZLED face)

Why had he been set free? What had made them change their minds so dramatically? Maybe he heard the full story later...Pilate's attempt to release a man named Jesus...the crowd calling for him (Barabbas) instead. Jesus going to die in his place, on the cross on which he should have been put to death.

Conclusion

Perhaps some of us have asked this same question: 'Why did Jesus have to die?' None of us has been as violent as Barabbas, but the Bible tells us that we have all done wrong in God's sight (Rom 3:23). 'Christ also died for sins once for all, the righteous for the unrighteous, that he might bring us to God.' (1 Pet 3:18). Jesus not only died in the place of Barabbas, he died in place of me. It is only through Christ's death on the Cross that we can come to God. Is your faith based on Christ crucified for you?

PETER BANNISTER
Bridgwater

22 Crosses

TEXT

Any passage about the crucifixion.

AIM

To show that the cross of Jesus shows up our sin, God's love, and the need for a decision.

PREPARATION

(I assume the use of an overhead projector for this talk, but it could be done in other ways.)

° Cut out a paper cross large enough to fill the screen, with each of the four 'arms' equal in length.

° Draw a page of an arithmetic exercise book, large enough to fill two-thirds of the screen. On it write the sum *2+2=5* and mark it wrong with a big red cross.

° Draw the inside of a Valentine card (I used Letraset—see p.17) large enough to fill two-thirds of the screen. Write on it *I love you passionately* and add dozens of kisses.

° Draw a cross-roads road-sign, large enough to fill two-thirds of the screen.

° Draw a picture of Jesus on the cross large enough to fill one-third of the screen.

PRESENTATION

(a) *Introduction*

Project the large cross on to the screen so that it appears as an X.
Then swivel it so that it appears as a + then swivel it again to an X.
Ask the audience to think of all the different ways we use that cross
shape (for multiplication, addition, error sign, Green Cross Code,
cross-roads, kiss, etc.) Say you're going to think about just three uses
of that cross shape.

(b) *The cross points to our sin*

Ask the (rhetorical) question, 'Are you (or were you) any good at
arithmetic at school?'

I was useless. My arithmetic exercise book was full of little crosses.
(Project the page from the exercise book.)

Ask: 'What did that cross tell me? Answer: 'You'd got it wrong!'
(Project the crucifixion picture on to another part of the screen.)

Jesus' cross marks our lives 'wrong'. It was because of our sins that
he died. Every time we say something we shouldn't: cross, wrong.
Every time we think something we shouldn't: cross, wrong. Every
time we fail to love God with our whole heart: cross, wrong.

(c) *The cross points to God's love*

Ask if they can remember Valentine's Day. Did they get cards? Most
of the Valentine cards that get sent have crosses on them. (Project the
picture of the Valentine card.) Were all those crosses saying that the
sender had got it wrong? Answer: 'No! They mean "I love you".'
(Project the crucifixion picture on to another part of the screen.)

Jesus' cross says 'I love you' as well—in a big way.

(d) *The cross demands a decision*

I remember when petrol was cheap and you could just go off for a
drive for the fun of it and soak up the scenery and relax. But then
you'd have to stir yourself because you came across one of these
things...(project the cross-roads picture) and you'd have to make a
decision.

The cross of Jesus is like that (project the crucifixion picture on to another part of the screen). It forces us to make a decision: are we going to go Jesus' way or our way?

If we know Jesus marks our lives wrong (like the cross in the exercise book) and that he loves us so much he was prepared to die for us (remember the Valentine card), then we'll surely want to go his way. But we've got to decide...

JOHN ANSCOMBE
Scripture Union

23 Easter Sunday mistakes

TEXT

Mk 16:1–8

AIM

To show that people can miss out on the reality of the resurrection because of the mistakes they make.

PREPARATION

Items you need are some embalming fluid (borrow from a local undertaker), some talc, after shave, hair spray, perfume. A large stone, a drawing or model of the empty tomb, a Gospel.

PRESENTATION

Tell the congregation to imagine there is an outing to the seaside—give date, time and place to meet. Someone gets there on a different day at a different time and wonders why no one else is there. They miss the fun of the outing because they have made mistakes. There were some mistakes on the first Easter Sunday.

(a) We use deodorants on our bodies while we are alive, to make them smell nice. (Produce talc, after shave, hair spray, perfume.) Some deodorants are used on bodies that have died. (Produce embalming fluid.) This is the kind of thing which would be used on the body of Jesus when he died. But this is where the first mistake also happened.

The mistake was made by the women who came with spices early

85

on Easter Sunday morning. For one thing, Joseph and Nicodemus had already done the job; and for another, Jesus was no longer dead. He didn't need the spices because he was alive.

(b) The women were concerned about the stone. (Produce stone.) Explain how it had been put in front of tomb and why. The women discussed the problem (v.3). They were unlikely to find anyone to help. But they need not have worried. Why? Refer to Mt 28:2. The stone had already been rolled away.

Problems can stop us appreciating reality of Jesus being alive. We think about them, discuss them and they go round and round in our minds. But if Jesus is alive we can take our problems to him!

(c) The sepulchre (name given to tomb) was where the third mistake was made. (Produce picture or show model.) They were looking in the sepulchre for Jesus, but he was not there as the two men (angels) explained (Lk 24:5). They looked in the wrong place. They looked back to what had happened in the past when Jesus died. Many people think Jesus is to do with the past. They have wrong idea about him. They think he is to do with musty-smelling churches (like tombs?), old, small-print black Bibles and people doing odd things in churches. So they miss out on the reality of Jesus being alive.

(d) Fourth mistake was to do with what the angel said (v.7) 'He is going...just as he told you.' Refer to Lk 24:6–7. Jesus had told them what would happen to him. Illustrate from Mk 14:28. Point out the mistake of not knowing the Scriptures. If we do not know the Scriptures, we miss out on the reality of the living Lord Jesus. Jesus is alive, today.

Don't miss out on the reality of it by making mistakes like these women who were concerned about the *spices*—things, the *stone*—-problems, the *sepulchre*—because they had the wrong idea and they didn't know the *Scriptures*. Rather know he is alive and Lord.

ALAN PUGMIRE
Manchester

24 An agent investigates—Easter

TEXT

Mt 28:1–15

AIM

To present evidence for the resurrection.

PREPARATION

An agent is to be employed by the Roman Emperor to investigate the Christian Movement. Enlist four clear-voiced adults to take the parts of the captain of the guard, Caiaphas, Mary from Magdala and Peter. The minister takes the part of the Agent.

Compose scripts from which they can read (as dramatically as possible). The scripts need to include a moderate number of supplementary questions by the Agent to avoid long speeches by the interviewees.

PRESENTATION

The Agent calls the interviewees up one by one to a spot some distance from him (so as to help them speak loudly).

Summary of script

The Captain of the guard is asked what happened after the body had been taken from the cross. He explains about the burial and placing of the guard.

Agent: 'What went wrong?'

The *Captain* explains that they dozed off after a heavy day's duty at Passover time.

Agent: 'Disgraceful—I'll have to talk to the chief priest about this...'.

The *Agent* respectfully informs *Caiaphas* that the guards slept on duty. *Caiaphas* explains they reported to him and were told to tell the story about the disciples stealing the body.

The *Agent* questions the morality of that. *Caiaphas* makes a weak excuse and asked to be informed of anything the *Agent* finds out.

The *Agent* asks *Mary* about her faith. She explains how she met Jesus. She points out that the soldiers would have been executed if they had really gone to sleep, and that she could not have imagined her meeting with Jesus because she was not expecting to meet him.

The *Agent*, only half believing her, protests that he must ask one of the men who followed Jesus, who would talk more sense.

Peter points out that even if the guards had been asleep they would have woken up if the disciples had tried to move the stone. They did not expect Jesus to rise again. They remembered Jesus saying that he would, but did not really believe him. Peter points out that if they had been telling lies they would not have been prepared to risk the wrath of the authorities (Acts 4) for their preaching about Jesus.

The *Agent* concludes by briefly summing up the evidence for the resurrection and indicating his own acceptance of it.

EDWARD PRATT
Derby

25 Easter table

TEXT

1 Cor 15:6

AIM

To show that Christianity has many proofs of its truth.

PREPARATION

Prepare the visual aid, which is basically a picture of an oblong table (as illustrated) made in such a way that you can assemble it bit by bit as your talk unfolds. Try to get the perspectives right by finding a suitable 'horizon spot' at which the parallel lines can meet. (Stick the pieces on with Blu-tack or whatever you like to use.)

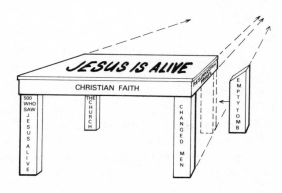

Take a pair of gloves and a small piece of bread with you into the pulpit. Ask some strong-minded member of the congregation to be ready to stand up at the beginning of your sermon to contradict you.

PRESENTATION

Start your sermon in the pulpit wearing a pair of gloves. Say emphatically: 'The Christian faith is true and Easter Day proves it' (put up *Easter Day*), at which your previously conscripted heckler shouts, 'I don't believe you! The Christian faith isn't true. It hasn't a leg to stand on.'

'Oh yes it has', you reply.

'Oh no it hasn't.'

'Oh yes it has' (etc.).

'All right then—prove it.'

'Right, I will. In fact I'll give you *four* legs.'

Take your gloves off obviously, leave them in the pulpit and come down to where your visual aid will be displayed. (If you work from the pulpit, leave your gloves on your seat.)

The Christian faith is based on the fact that Jesus is alive. (Put up the table top with *Christian Faith* on the front.) Add *Jesus is Alive* to the top and then explain that Jesus showed himself alive to his followers and gave them infallible, sure, proofs of his Resurrection (put up *Resurrection Proofs*). What are some of the proofs?

(a) *Empty tomb*

When Jesus rose from the dead he came out of the tomb and left it empty. 'Will one of you go into the pulpit please?—Is it empty?—I'm not there, but it is not quite empty—my gloves are in there.' Jesus left his shroud, his grave clothes, but, like my gloves, they were empty too.

(b) *500 who saw Jesus alive*

Mary Magdalene saw Jesus, other women too; two disciples at Emmaus, then ten in the upper room watched him eating bread; later the eleven, then 500 saw him at once. What a number of witnesses! How many are there here?—20 50 100 300? (Ask a child to come out and give him a small piece of bread to eat.) Who saw it? Is he alive? Is he a ghost?

(c) *Changed men*

When the disciples knew Jesus was alive again their lives were changed. Peter was afraid; after, he was bold. Thomas was sceptical; after, he was certain. This last week...(tell of someone you know whose life was changed).

(d) *The church*

Look at this church building. It is here because Jesus lives. But even more important, 20 100 300 people are gathered. All over the world hundreds of millions of Christians are gathering together to worship the risen Christ. It MUST be true—it is TRUE.

So the Christian faith has at least four legs to stand on. Don't let anyone dissuade you or try to blind you with science or any false arguments. 'Has the Christian faith got a let to stand on? Oh yes it has!'

PETER BARTON
Malmesbury

26 Mary Magdalene's tears

TEXT

Jn 20:11–18

AIM

To show how we are often blinded from recognizing Jesus, but that if we really love him, we will find him.

PREPARATION

Flannelgraph or teazleboard figures: the rising sun, an eastern house, the three crosses, the empty tomb, a woman standing. Words on three cards: *Tears hide from God's word; Tears keep us from Jesus; Tears lead us to Jesus.*

PRESENTATION

Tell the story of the first Easter Day. Set the scene with the use of the figures as given above, ending with the figure of the woman (Mary). Refer to Jn 20:11 where we have the opening words, 'But Mary'.

(a) Have you ever felt that others have an easy time in life? Have you ever felt that you are the one who battles on, often unnoticed, and seem to miss the joy and excitement that others have? Then you are just like Mary! Over the years she had done so much for Jesus, but now she was on her own while others knew that Jesus was alive.

Tell a little of the background of Mary; how she had ministered to Jesus during his three years of ministry, how she was one of the few who had stayed at the cross to the end, and how she had seen where his body had been laid and was now by the tomb early on Sunday morning.

Tell also how she wasn't the first there, that Easter morning—the group of women had seen and received the angels' message; Peter and John too had been there, and John had believed that Jesus was alive. The others had seen and some had believed, but Mary.... We can see her standing by the tomb weeping, tears streaming down her face, she had loved Jesus so much!

(b) Those tears did three things for Mary:

° They hid God's messengers (vv.12–13). Go over the incident stressing that Mary was crying so much that she didn't even notice that these men were angels. Luke tells us that the other women believed and acted on the message of the angels at the tomb. They were sent by God, but Mary didn't listen.

How easy it is to become so blinded by our own sorrow or difficulty, that we never understand what God is trying to teach us through his messengers, other Christians who are trying to share with us, God's written word, the Bible. (Put up card *Tears hide from God's word.*)

° They kept her from Jesus himself, for a time (vv.14–15). Go over the incident, stressing that she had already made up her mind that Jesus was dead, and that her own sorrow blinded her from the facts.

How sad that some people today have already made up their minds that although Jesus was a wonderful man who gave us some great teaching, he couldn't have come alive again. They have in many ways become so blinded by the sufferings of mankind (refugees, wars, cancer, divorce etc.) that they have not seen that Jesus really is alive all the time. (Put up card *Tears keep us from Jesus.*)

° Mary's tears, were also tears of love for Jesus, so that in the end they led her to Jesus (v.16). Go over the remainder of the incident.

(c) It's very wonderful, but so very true, that all who really love God and want to know the truth about Jesus, will in the end find him. Jesus once said 'Those who seek (me) shall find (me)'. (Put up card *Tears lead us to Jesus.*) This Easter, don't let anything hide you or keep you away from Jesus; but know for sure that he rose from the dead and is alive for ever!

GARRY GUINNESS
Watford

27 Easter with 0008! (Treble 0 8)

Text

1 Cor 15:3,4

Aim

Using the storyteller's art to present the truths of Good Friday and Easter with a vivid freshness.

Preparation

0008 is the name of a glove puppet with five stubby fingers for legs, a bulbous head and moving button eyes. Sold commercially as Olly Octopus, in Christian hands it becomes a new creature!

This puppet is a silent one—which greatly helps preachers of limited ventriloquist ability—and depends upon activity to communicate (cf Emu). In the pulpit appropriate waggling of legs and shaking up and down movements signify excitement, impatience, agreement, while sideways movements portray sadness, anger, disagreement, 'no' to questions etc., depending on speed and context.

Once bought or constructed he can be introduced very simply in almost any talk for a short spot-appearance. His speciality is intelligence. He has agents literally everywhere, for 0008 is Super-Spy, the master-mind of the worldwide spider network, to whom every spider reports what they have spied. He can therefore usefully report on all the sorts of sins that go on in what most people believe to be the secrecy of kitchen, bedroom etc. He also has a computer memory bank store of all that past generations of spiders have reported, a faculty upon which the following presentation draws. The presentation can be broken into three separate presentations if thought desirable.

Presentation

I promised my friend 0008 would be here today...for those who don't know he is a 'Super Spy'. A 'Spy-der'. Have you noticed spiders are just everywhere? They make excellent agents. Treble 0 8 is special. He has lost three legs hence the treble 0. Spiders normally have 8 legs. He's very silent. Spiders don't bark like dogs or miaow like cats. He whispers or projects thought images.

Ah! He wants me to get on with it! He wants to tell you what his agent ancestors and relatives experienced many years ago! The story of Easter through spiders' eyes!

(In presenting each of the following reports remember that it is 0008's story and there should therefore be appropriate pauses for the preacher to check with 0008 that he is telling it right and for 0008 to whisper or nod agreement. An OHP can be used to portray pictures of the historic agents at cross, tomb, upper room, and 0008 can show interest in this with excitement, sadness being exhibited where appropriate.)

(a) *The report of agent VIII (V-treble-1)*

V-treble-1 was a small spider who travelled with the Roman legions.

His home was a small crack in the wooden shaft of a Roman spear. He could hide under the metal and be quite safe in the fiercest battle and he could peep out with a grandstand view when his soldier was on the march or on duty.

And so it was that he came to be perched on that green hill outside Jerusalem, peeping out he saw the crowds, and the three men crucified. Nothing very unusual about that for him—a sight he often saw. But then he started to notice differences.... The man on the middle cross didn't look like a criminal, and he hadn't cursed or sworn when they nailed him to the wood. He'd said '*Father, forgive them they know not what they do*'. Then after a while it became strangely dark...it made one's hairs stand up...spooky...and he'd heard the man called Jesus cry out '*My God, my God, why have you forsaken me*' and then...there was the earthquake...and then he had to scuttle for cover.

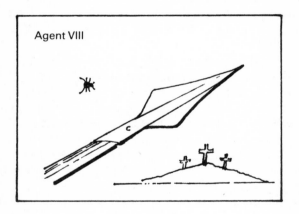

Agent VIII

His soldier's spear had been thrust deep into the side of Jesus, and there was the redness of blood everywhere. It was the real stuff, but he didn't make a meal of it like he usually did. Instead he felt as if a great flood of love had poured all over him.

'God so loved the world that he gave his only Son that people should not perish but have eternal life'.

God's Son Jesus dying for men's sins....

No wonder there was darkness, and earthquakes and...love.

(b) *The report of agent IIX (Double 1-X)*

This agent hadn't been born with 10 legs and lost 2. It was just that for the size of his body he *seemed* to have more and was always tripping over himself. Double 1-X was an immigrant—Roman by place of birth but widely travelled and he'd now settled down in a quiet secluded garden. He enjoyed moving amongst the grasses and sunning himself in sheltered crevices in the rock. But early one morning the peace of his retirement was shattered. His sleeping quarters were in a cave entered (by him) through a very small crevice. They had buried a body there a day or two earlier. Nothing unusual in that. It was what the cave had been made for.

But Double 1-X woke with a start—the corpse had begun to glow and then the glow had detached itself from the clothes and moved out through the walls. Double 1-X scuttled through his narrow crevice, just large enough for a spider, to the outside. Yes! There was the glow, but no it wasn't a glow, it was a man! It was the man who had been dead and wrapped up in the cave.

Agent IIX

Then the earth shook and an angel appeared and the stone across the entrance to the cave fell flat. The soldiers guarding the cave had frozen at first; now they ran for their lives. And then the angels moved inside the cave and the figure of the man faded into the faintness of a gentle glow hardly visible.

Then women came fearfully and tearfully. They didn't seem to understand...but then they hadn't seen all he had seen.

This had never been seen before...not ever....

This was a resurrection!

(c) *The report of agent 0 (Thēta)*

A house spider living in the city of Jerusalem. Greek because so many people spoke Greek in those days and named *Thēta* because that is the eighth letter in the Greek alphabet.

Thēta had gone into hiding just before the Jewish passover to avoid the annual spring-clean and had now moved back to witness some very strange things.

First there had been this very strange party with Jesus and his disciples with the one called Judas suddenly rushing out; and they had become all solemn eating some bread and drinking some wine because Jesus had said it was his body and his blood. How strange 0 thought.

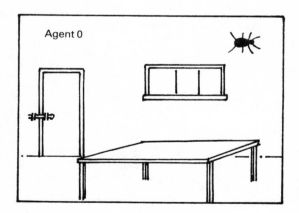

Then they had all gone out, even though it was night. And then they had all come back later on, but one at a time mainly, all out of breath and very frightened, all except Peter and John and...Jesus. And ladies joined them and they locked the doors and looked done in.

Later Peter and John joined them.

Then, Sunday morning, the ladies had gone off together very early...and then Mary Magdalene rushed back; and then Peter and John rushed out with her. They came back a bit later, and there was lots of talk about an empty tomb and meeting Jesus; but they were all confused, not knowing what to think or make of it. That very same night suddenly Jesus appeared out of thin air. It really was him... It was unbelievable...He was the same but different. And Jesus began to explain.... He made them look very carefully at what the scriptures said.

Ah! Yes! 0008 there's something important you want to tell everyone? (Listen for a moment to imagined whispers.)

Ah! Yes! He says you're not just to rely on what his ancestor agents reported. He says it is very important to read what the apostles wrote down in the Bible. What the Bible says is very, very, accurate and explains why Jesus died and rose again.

Quote 1 Cor 15:3, 4.

STEWART SYMONS
Liverpool

28 Ascension promises

TEXT

Acts 1:1–11, see also Jn 14:3, 16–17

AIM

To show that two very important promises were made at the time of
the Ascension concerning the coming of the Holy Spirit and the return
of Jesus.

In the talk that follows it is assumed that it will be given on the
Sunday after the Ascension. It might be quite easily adapted to be
given during the Advent season.

PREPARATION

Obtain or draw (possibly for use on an OHP) a picture of a space
rocket. Make a large return rail ticket with the words *Earth to Heaven*
and *Heaven to Earth*. 'Clip' the former part. Make eleven large cards
that can be held up by children so that all the congregation can see the
numbers written on them. Two of the cards will need to be larger than
the others. On ten of the cards have the numbers one to ten. On the
back of the first card either have the words *Holy Spirit* or have a picture
depicting the Spirit such as a flame or a dove. On the eleventh card
have a large question mark, and on the back *Coming soon Jesus*. Have
the means of making a loud noise! Have a mock up newspaper with
headline *JESUS CHRIST RETURNED YESTERDAY*.

PRESENTATION

Showing the rocket, talk about launching it by countdown. Involving ten children call out the numbers from ten to one and get each child to raise their number above their head. Immediately after one is raised sound the loud noise.

Explain that at the time of the Ascension when Jesus returned to his Father in heaven two count-downs began, both of which looked forward to events that were promised would happen sooner or later; there was:

(a) *The countdown to Pentecost (The coming of the Holy Spirit)*

Repeat the count-down using the cards, but when reaching the last card ask the child holding it to turn it round, revealing *Holy Spirit* (or illustration). Explain how Jesus promised that he would be sent shortly after Jesus returned to heaven (see Acts 1:4–5, 8; Jn 14:16–17). He actually came *ten* days after Jesus left on the day we call Whitsunday or Pentecost.

(b) *The countdown to the Parousia (The second coming of Jesus)*

Now we have a big problem, because though there is a day when Jesus will return we cannot do the count-down because Jesus has not told us when it is. Get a child to hold up the eleventh card with the question mark, then to turn it round to reveal *Coming soon Jesus*. Perhaps quote from Acts 1:6–7 and Mt 24:36.

° *Why do Christians believe Jesus is coming back?* Show the giant rail ticket and explain that the first half has been used (hence the 'clip'), but it is not a single ticket. The return half has not yet been used. We know it will be, even though we do not know when, because he promised (Jn 14:3) and so did the angels (Acts 1:10–11). In his life on earth Jesus told his disciples that he would be crucified (he was); that he would rise from the dead and ascend to his Father (he did); that he would send the Holy Spirit (he came); that there would be a church (there is). Jesus keeps his promises. Just because he has not returned yet does not mean that he will not.

° *What will happen when Jesus returns?* Such an event is surely to be newsworthy. Do you think we might see headlines like this: *JESUS*

CHRIST RETURNED YESTERDAY? Draw out the point that when Jesus comes it will be the end of the world, so there will be no more newspapers, but Christians will go to be with the Lord to be rewarded according to how they used their lives. Others will be judged for their sins.

° *What difference does Jesus's promise to return make now?* Compare the difference of looking forward to a friend who is (say) returning from abroad and a rent collector. (See Mt 24:45 – 25:13; 2 Pet 3:10ff).

ANDREW HETHERINGTON
Bootle

MICHAEL BOTTING
Editor

29 What's new? A talk for Whitsunday

To explain what was new for mankind when the Holy Spirit was poured out at Pentecost.

PREPARATION

Arrange for different members of the congregation to read the following texts: (1) Joel 2:28–29, (2) Jer 31:31–34, (3) Ezek 36:26–27, (4) Is 12:1–2. Have on two pieces of card covered with teazlegraph material the letters *Tri* and *Unity*. Cut out from different coloured day-glo card three figures like the 'Mr Therm' men and print across their middles *Tom, Dick* and *Harry*. Make from card two 'tables' to represent the stone tables for the ten commandments. Cut out of day-glo card (in pink or red) a heart shape, some enlarged musical notes (or people obviously praising), on white card a picture of an open Bible, on pink card a picture of praying hands, on any colour card a picture of a gift (decorative string can be put round it) and on yellow card cut out eight shapes that look like tongues of fire. On all these visuals stick velcro, ready for use on the teazlegraph board.

PRESENTATION

Refer to the Creed said in the service. Who did we say we believed in? Draw out the word Trinity and using the cards with *Tri* and *Unity* show how the word was derived. Explain that in a sense we are each trinities of body, mind and spirit.

Ask if the congregation think God has always existed, and Jesus the Son, and what about the Holy Spirit? Draw out that though the Holy Spirit has always existed, yet we do not hear much about him in the Old Testament.

Ask what is special about Whitsunday and what happened on the first Whitsunday? The Holy Spirit has always been around, yet on the first Whitsunday he was sent to the Church. What was new about his coming?

(a) *He comes to anyone*

Normally one had to be a very special person in Old Testament days to have God's Spirit: prophet, king, specially wise or very artistic. He was promised to the nation generally, but not to the individual particularly. Moses longed that all God's people might be prophets. But Joel made the wonderful prophecy (1) quote. So the Spirit is now for all, i.e. for Tom, Dick and Harry. He's for everyone in this church today, just for the asking. If we repent of sin and ask Jesus to be Saviour, we are promised the gift of the Spirit. (Place 'tongues of fire' over the heads of the three figures of Tom, Dick and Harry on the teazlegraph board.)

(b) *He comes into our lives*

In the Old Testament days God gave his people the ten commandments (put up table of stone on board). If they obeyed all would be well. The trouble was that they did not obey because they had no power within themselves to do so. Quote (2) and (3). (Put up the heart with the 'tongue' in the centre of it.) The quotations spoke of God coming to live within us by his Spirit. Refer to William Temple's famous observation that he could not compose music like Beethoven or paint pictures like Turner without the spirit of those artists coming to live within him. Nor could he live a life like Jesus without the Spirit of Jesus coming within him, but that was what God promised him could happen.

(c) *He comes in fullness*

No one in former days knew anything like the experience of the Spirit that the early church came to know. Isaiah had some vision of it, quote (4). Use the remaining visual aids with 'tongues' over each to illustrate:
° A new sense of worship and praise
° A new ability to understand the Scriptures
° A new depth in prayer
° New gifts for all: tongues, prophecy, healing, wisdom, discernment, ministry.

Does everyone here know the infilling of the Spirit?

MICHAEL BOTTING
Editor

30 Pentecost (1)

Acts 2:1–4

AIM

To show the means of receiving the Holy Spirit, who is everywhere, and harnessing that gift for Christian service.

PREPARATION

You will need a battery-operated portable radio.

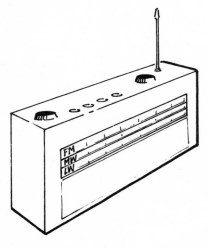

PRESENTATION

Ask the congregation to be quiet, telling them that the church is full of noise. Eventually it will go very quiet indeed. Tell them that you can still hear noise!

Tell them the church is full of speaking and music, but, of course, they cannot hear it. Then produce the radio.

After showing that there are no wires going to the radio, you can prove that the church is full of noise by switching on. The radio makes the noise which is all around us become audible.

Application

(a) The Holy Spirit, like the unheard noise, is all around us.

(b) There is the need to switch on, and that is done by asking God to fill us with his Holy Spirit, who is otherwise not experienced.

(c) Once 'switched on' we need to tune in to a particular channel as if to hear a programme. Our tuning is through prayer, Bible-reading, meeting with other Christians, corporate worship, the sacraments and study. These are the channels by which God comes to us.

(d) Another effect of switching on the radio is that if we turn up the volume, others can hear it as well as ourselves. If we 'switch on' to God, and 'tune in' sincerely, then others will benefit by the love of God which will flow through us.

BOB METCALF
Liverpool

31 Pentecost (2)

TEXT

Acts 10:44

AIM

To show that the Holy Spirit gives life and enthusiasm.

PREPARATION

A sparklet soda syphon is required, with a small sparklet bottle of gas available.

PRESENTATION

(a) Show the children the syphon. They will tell you that it needs to be full of soda water. Fill it with water and they will think it is ready for use. To all intents and purposes, it is so. Invite a child to squirt it at someone, possibly yourself. Nothing happens.

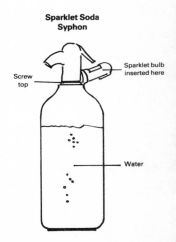

Sparklet Soda Syphon

Screw top

Sparklet bulb inserted here

Water

Tell the audience that this is like the Church where there is no life. The people are present, but there is no real enthusiasm for the work of God, and for his joyful worship.

(b) Now, insert the sparklet gas bottle, and release the gas into the syphon. The

108

operation this time needs to be controlled, but the water becomes full of life and will squirt readily and effervesce.

This is like the same Church, responding to the teaching of the Holy Spirit, coming alive, interesting and enthusiastic in its mission.

BOB METCALF
Liverpool

32 The Holy Spirit and a glove

TEXT

Jn 14:16–17 (GNB)

AIM

To show how we are powerless without the Holy Spirit.

PREPARATION

An ordinary glove which fits your hand.

PRESENTATION

(a) Say you have brought something which you hope you do not need. (Produce your glove.) You hope it will not be so cold in church! But it reminds you of some people. Not much use! Glove is a floppy thing (wave around). It cannot pick things up, hold them or wave very well.

Ask how you can make it useful. Someone might tell you to put it on. (Put your hand in it; show how your hand fills it.) The Bible tells us to *be filled* with the Holy Spirit. When a hand fills a glove it takes control of the glove. When Holy Spirit fills our lives he takes control of them.

(b) What happens to a hand when in glove? It is *invisible*. The Holy Spirit is invisible. Refer to Jn 14:17 'The world...cannot see him'. In Acts 2 we are told the Holy Spirit is like the wind. The wind is invisible, but you can see the effects of it by trees blowing. When the Holy Spirit works you can see the effects (move fingers around) even though you can't see him. He is still real, e.g. the person you speak to on a telephone is invisible to you, but is still real.

(c) The glove cannot pick things up itself. But when a hand is in it, it can do so. The Holy Spirit is a *Helper* who can help us to do things we cannot do ourselves. Refer to Jn 14:16 'he will give you another helper'. He helps us in our worship, to pray, read the Bible and tell others about Jesus.

(d) If someone asks the way, the glove cannot show it on its own. But with a hand inside, the glove can point. It can therefore be a *guide*. The Holy Spirit is a Guide. Refer to Jn 14:17 'He is the Spirit who reveals the truth about God', i.e. he guides us in our understanding about God.

The Holy Spirit is one who is in you, invisible, a Helper and a Guide. End with text.

ALAN PUGMIRE
Manchester

33 The fruit of the Spirit

TEXT

Gal 5:22f (GNB)

AIM

To show how a Christian may be recognised.

PREPARATION

Prepare nine card badges, nice and colourful, each to represent one of the qualities listed in the passage. With the exception of *'Humility'* all the badges should be large, so that they can be seen and together will cover the body of a volunteer. Some means of attaching them to the volunteer should be provided: double-sided sellotape on the back of the badges works well. Some suggested designs appear below. It will help to have also two or three large conventional badges and a piece of fruit.

PRESENTATION

Show your conventional badges (if you have them) and ask to see any that people might be wearing. Why do people wear badges? Someone's badge may tell us who he is, what he does, what his interests are.

Badges can tell us a lot. How can you tell a Christian? Ideas?

Jesus said that you can tell whether or not someone is a Christian by his fruit (Mt 7:20). What did he mean? Do Christians go around with a banana around their neck or an orange stuck on their jumper? (Demonstrate with your piece of fruit for a laugh!)

Ask for a volunteer to stand beside you as you go through the Galatians passage. Take each fruit in turn (GNB used here) and explain it briefly. You may find the following breakdown helpful:

The most important ones: *Love, Joy, Peace.*

The way we act towards others: *Patience, Kindness, Goodness.*

Qualities in ourselves: *Faithfulness, Humility, Self-control.*

(As you come to each fruit, take the relevant badge and fix it to your volunteer. By the end the arms, legs and head should be covered.)

All these things are the fruit of the Spirit. By them we may recognise a Christian. Look at your volunteer: wearing all of the badges.

Are you wearing them all too?

STEVEN FOSTER
Redditch

34 Revival (Whitsunday)

TEXT

Ezek 37:1–14

AIM

To teach how the church can be revived and to stress the need for a balance between emphasis on the word and the Spirit.

PREPARATION

Prepare for the teazlegraph board the words *How is the Church to be revived? Hear the* WORD *of God*, and *Receive the* WIND *of God*. The WORD could be written on the background of an open Bible and WIND could have a letter each on four simple kites cut out of different colours of day-glo paper, with short lengths of string trailing from them. (This was particularly appropriate when this talk was given its first airing, because the Family Service was followed by a church picnic at which there was a kite-flying competition.) Also cut out of white paper lots of bones and skulls.

PRESENTATION

Refer to people being taken into slavery, illustrating with modern examples such as the Jews in Nazi Germany. Then refer back to about 600 BC when Ezekiel was prophesying. He had a vision, a kind of dream with a definite message. He saw a valley, or plain, with many skeletons on the ground. The bones were very dry, implying that they had been there a long time. Ask what that might mean and draw out that they represented Israel and Judah who had been depressed and hopeless for ten years. (Put up bones and skulls at bottom of board.)

Ezekiel heard a voice—Ezekiel, can these bones live? Ask whose voice? Ezekiel thought that the obvious answer was 'no', so why ask? Perhaps God had a message of hope. He replied, 'O Lord God, you know'.

(a) *Hear the* WORD *of God*

Tell the story in vv. 4–8 and put up the words on the board about a quarter of the way down. Ask if the army lived? What was still needed?

(b) *Receive the* WIND *of God*

Continue the story in vv.9–10 and explain about the need for breath. Perhaps refer to Adam being created by God, but still needing breath to bring him to life. Refer to the four winds which meant the four corners of the earth. Explain that the words *breath, wind* and *spirit* are all the same word in Hebrew. In Greek *wind* and *spirit* are the same word *pneuma* from which we get words like *pneumatic*. The army had to receive the *WIND of God* (put up words on the board.) This was a message to the whole nation. One day there would be revival and the united nation would return to its own country.

What does it have to say to us in the church? Many churches in our land seem lifeless and hopeless, which is why so many are increasingly empty. It has been said that if the Holy Spirit left the church 90% of what the church does would continue to happen without anyone noticing!

Perhaps tell the story of a cemetery that had to restrict the number being buried in it to the local parish only. A notice was erected. '*This cemetery is for the dead living in this parish*'! Comment that there are many dead living in our parishes: 'dead in trespasses and sins' and perhaps there are some here.

(c) *How is the Church to be revived?*
   (Put up these words at top of the board)

Refer to the two statements below this question and comment along these lines: *Word of God*: the need for biblical preaching, home Bible study groups and private Bible reading to discover what God's word means to us today. *Wind of God*: it is not enough to know God's word, we have to be living it. The original disciples knew Jesus' word to them, but they did not live it till after receiving the Spirit at Pentecost.

We have to be open to the Spirit of God as a church that we may receive all his gifts and show forth his fruit of love, joy peace....then we shall know revivial. It could begin today.

MICHAEL BOTTING
Editor

35 The eternal triangle

Aɪᴍ

To show God as Father, Son and Holy Spirit.

Pʀᴇᴘᴀʀᴀᴛɪᴏɴ

Prepare flannelgraph or teazlegraph board
Triangles of all shapes and sizes.
A big equilateral triangle with GOD printed across it.
Three pieces of card: *Father—the Creator*
Son—Jesus the Saviour
Holy Spirit—the Helper.

Pʀᴇsᴇɴᴛᴀᴛɪᴏɴ

(Place a triangle on board)—discover its name—three angles—trio
means three—drop the 'o' and we have triangle. All shapes and
sizes—(place other triangles on board)—whichever way you look at
them they are still triangles. (Remove triangles. Place special triangle
on board.) Here we have a triangle with God written on it. We are
going to think about God in three different ways, but there is only one
God.

God as Father (place 'Father' card at one of the angles)

In the book of Genesis we read how God was there at the beginning
and made the world—he created everything 'And saw that it was
good'. He created Man in his own image. He gave people free-will—
the right to choose. But people did wrong things—they sinned and so

lost their fellowship with God. Even so God still loved the people, so he had to take some action to restore the relationship.

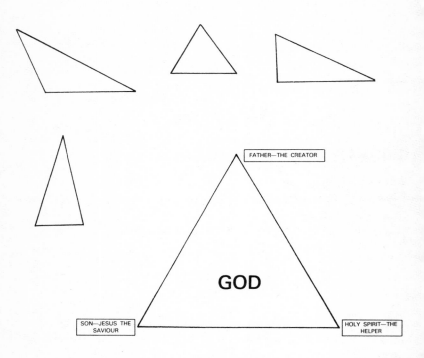

God as Son (place 'Son' card at another angle)

He sent his Son Jesus into the world. Jesus taught the people about the kingdom of God—he proclaimed the gospel—the good news. He showed the people what God was really like. 'He who has seen me has seen the Father.' Some people were angry—and they put Jesus to death on a cross. Jesus died that we might be forgiven for all the wrong things we have done. He died to put us right with God. Then on the first Easter morning Jesus rose from the dead and so conquered sin and returned in glory to God the Father.

118

God as Holy Spirit (place 'Holy Spirit' on the other angle)

God then sent his Holy Spirit into the world to help the disciples—in fact to change the disciples from men of fear to men of great courage so they could proclaim the good news of the kingdom.

This power is still available to us today. God can send his Holy Spirit to be our Helper to change us from people of fear to people of courage, proclaiming the Good News of the Kingdom just where we are today.

Conclusion

Our 'God' triangle needs the three equal angles to keep it whole. The Father as the Creator: the Son as Jesus the Saviour: the Holy Spirit as the Helper. Three persons but one God.

MYRTLE POCOCK
Keynsham, Bristol

36 The Trinity

Mk 1:10, 11.

Aim
To understand what is meant by the Trinity.

Preparation
Refer to *Mere Christianity* by C. S. Lewis, Part 4 *Beyond Personality*, chapter 2 'The Three-Personal God'. Produce large brightly-coloured drawing of Rubik Cube; and/or have an actual Rubik Cube to display as speaking.

Presentation
Talk about the puzzle that Rubik Cube can create. Produce cube, pointing out that each side is a different colour, but the cube is still a whole.

Just as many people make a jumble of Rubik Cube, so many Christians get in a muddle trying to understand and explain the Trinity. Although it is an essential part of the Christian faith, it is easier *seen* than *explained*. (Is 55:8—God is infinitely greater than we are. We cannot expect to understand him.)

Father, Son and Holy Spirit are distinct
Taking C. S. Lewis' illustration in *Beyond Personality* of a cube, hold up the Rubik Cube. The cube has six faces—each face separate and

different yet each one aspect of the whole cube. Not six cubes but one! From the top we could call it Yellow Cube. From the side Red Cube. From the bottom Green Cube. Still only one cube.

A very inadequate picture of God! But it helps to see the tri-unity of God. Avoid the error of thinking of God as an actor appearing in three different roles. From one angle he appears to be the Father, from another, the Son, from another, the Holy Spirit. Sometimes we can see two sides at once, and occasionally, all three, as in our text, or at our Lord's baptism.

Mark 1:10, 11 shows clearly the separate individuality of Father, Son and Holy Spirit when Jesus was baptized, the Father spoke, and the Holy Spirit descended (Mt 28:19; 2 Cor 13:14).

Repeat: The three Persons of the Trinity must be kept distinct— because there is relationship between them.

Father, Son and Holy Spirit share the same life

We must avoid regarding the Trinity as three separate gods. Refer to *Ground of Truth* by David Winter (Falcon) p.25ff. Acknowledging that any analogy stretched overmuch is capable of teaching heresy, Winter gives a helpful illustration:

In the Brown family, there is a father, mother and son. Each of them is equally a 'Brown'—in his or her own right. Collectively they are the Brown family. The father is superior in rank or seniority to his son—though the son has as much right to the family name as his father or mother.

With care we might think of God the Father, God the Son and God the Holy Spirit as three members of the 'God-family'—the Godhead. Each equally God, each fully divine, each with all the dignities and attributes of divinity. But God the Father is Head of the family—'The creation of the world is his through the Spirit and his Son' (Gen 1:1–2; Jn 1:3; Heb 1:2).

But, as Winter admits, the weakness of this illustration lies here: the *Brown family* consists of three separate people, each having independent existence. The *Godhead* shares not only the same characteristics and the closest ties (like the Browns at the human level) but *the same life* as well.

Emphasise (in the light of the above contrast between Browns and the Godhead) that it is not so much of a contradiction to speak of 'three in one', i.e. three persons but one God; point out that children at school know perfectly well that three ones do *not* necessarily make three—it's important to use the right sign between the ones! Things which are quite separable from one another,—e.g. three planets; three toffees; three footballs—these require the *plus* (+) sign. But when things indwell one another—e.g. length and breadth and height—these can only be multiplied, in which case, the three together make *one*!

Conclusion

The three Persons of the Trinity, though distinct, are revealed in Scripture as being so mutually indwelt that, if we are to apply arithmetic to them at all, we cannot add, but only multiply them together. Then, if each is ONE, the three together are ONE!

1x1x1=1

In presenting part of this material, the author has dug out some well-worn notes, the 'source' of which he thinks is Prebendary Gordon Harman. If this is the case, then it is hoped that there is sufficient accuracy in what is here reproduced, and renewed appreciation of his 'original' thinking is expressed to Gordon Harman.

GARTH GRINHAM
Southport

37 Living Water—A harvest sermon

TEXT

Jn 4:1–30.

AIM

To show the ways in which we need Jesus as Living Water.

PREPARATION

Collect a shopping bag with some items (eggs, butter, flour, corn flakes, orange squash). A washing-up bowl, a watering can and a glass of water are also needed.

PRESENTATION

Ask if anyone ever goes shopping. Say you have been and empty your bag, mentioning something about each item. We need food or we will die. What else do we need? Possible answers include clothes, money, roof, water, friends, work. Which is most important?

Refer to saying 'The best things in life are free'. Talk about water. If someone mentions water rates, point out you can put a bucket out in the rain! Mention that Jesus once wanted water because he was thirsty. He hoped to get it from Jacob's well. Ask if they know who else wanted water? Samaritan woman.

Explain how conversation began and how unusual it was for a Jew and Samaritan to talk. Refer to what Jesus said in Jn 4:10. What does the water that Jesus gives do?

Bowl

Used for washing dishes, clothes or self. Woman in story had done wrong things and needed to be made clean. Refer to Jesus cleansing from sin.

Watering can

We don't use this to wash plants! We use it to feed them to keep them alive. We depend on water for life. 'Living water' Jesus promised to woman would give life. Jesus gives us new life.

Glass

This contains the kind of thing Jesus asked for. A drink satisfies your thirst. Jesus said that whoever drank of the water he gave would never thirst again. He satisfies. Many try to find satisfaction in other things, but they still want more because the other things don't satisfy.

Water is a harvest gift from God though we don't often think of it in that way. It reminds us of Jesus—the Living Water who makes us clean, gives life and satisfies us.

Scripture Union Choruses No.79 could be used to end. 'I'm feeding on the Living Bread.'

ALAN PUGMIRE
Manchester

38 The feast of tabernacles— A harvest sermon

Text
Deut 16:13–17, Jn 8:12, 7:37–39.

Aim
To use the Jewish Feast of Tabernacles to bring deeper understanding to our Christian harvest festival.

Preparation

This talk is not for the accident-prone speaker without a *reasonable imagination!*

Allowing plenty of time, build in a prominent position, possibly on a small stage, a miniature tabernacle or booth. The structure can be two clothes horses, though it can be pointed out that the fourth side would normally be against a house wall. The main features should be plenty of fresh leaves, some citrus fruit like lemons, oranges and grapefruit and that the structure is open to the sky. You should have a candle in a holder and matches available.

If there is enough space at the front of the church erect the teazle-graph board. Add the main headings below in a variety of colours, e.g. orange, red and green respectively. Pictures of a sheaf of corn, a cross and a well for water, with velcro on the back could also be available.

Presentation

Refer to the tabernacle and explain that the 'Feast of Tabernacles' was one of the Hebrew (or Jewish) harvest festivals. Put the citrus fruit in a conspicuous position around the tabernacle, explaining that they are more common in Israel than our apples and pears. Mention that the tabernacle would be open to the sky, could be as big as 12 by 10 feet, or even seat 100 people and people sometimes lived in them for a week (in October). Ask why God told the people to build tabernacles, and what they could mean to us as Christians. (If you use the teazlegraph board put up the word *Tabernacle* at the top and then the first main heading.)

(a) *Thanksgiving for harvest*

Refer to the fruit and explain that the feast was really very similar to our harvest festival. It was a time of great joy, the Temple treasury was refilled, good things were shared out to the poor. (Place picture of sheaf of corn on board alongside heading.)

(b) *Release from slavery*

This feast was commanded by God from the time that the children of Israel came out of their slavery in Egypt and wandered in the wilderness for 40 years, living in tents.

Ask in what way we are in slavery. Draw out that we are slaves to sin. Then ask how we are released from sin and speak of the cross. (Put up the cross opposite the heading.)

As the feast developed over the years, various customs became linked with it, and two are referred to in John's Gospel.

°*Light* – The great candelabra in the temple Court of the Women was lit to represent the fire in the wilderness which guided the children of Israel by night. These four great lights in the temple shone out over the city of Jerusalem. This was done every night, but not on the last night of the feast.

Suddenly, as the sun was setting, Jesus spoke out to all the people aware of the gloom 'I am the light of the world'.

Explain that he is the One to show us the way to God and guide us in our daily living. (Light the candle by the model tabernacle.)

(c) *Praise for the gift of rain*

This custom was not commanded by God, but grew up after the Exile and was utilised by Jesus on the last great day of the feast.

° *Water* – Refer to the procession of priests down to the pool of Siloam, all dressed in white robes, collecting water in golden vases and carrying it to the temple gates where it would be poured out. They would sing 'With joy you will draw water from the wells of salvation' (Is 12:3).

This was performed on seven days, but not on the eighth day. At the moment on the eighth day when it would have been done, Jesus steps forward and offers better water than Siloam: 'If any one thirst, let him come to me and drink'. Explain briefly his meaning from Jn 7:37–39 concerning the Holy Spirit.

Refer to the much greater thankfulness for water in parts of the world like Israel, than in Britain. (Put up well alongside heading.) Just as the Hebrews came to give thanks for rain poured out on them by God at their Feast of Tabernacles, we should give God thanks that he has poured out his Spirit on all those who have received Jesus as Saviour from sin.

MICHAEL BOTTING
Editor

39 Take root and bear fruit—
A harvest sermon

TEXT

2 Kings 19:29–30.

AIM

To illustrate the Christian life by means of a fruitful tree.

PREPARATION

Get a good artist to paint on a large sheet of white cardboard a healthy-looking tree with its roots visible. Stick on the tree near the top, in the middle and near the bottom of the foliage, three fruit-like shapes, possibly in day-glo red. With a sharp Stanley-type blade cut out four rectangles each three to four inches wide and long enough for the four words *Jesus, Repentance, Spirit* and *Soul* printed on an under sheet of card to show through the gaps. One of the rectangles should be in the roots of the tree to reveal *Jesus* underneath. The other three should each carry one of the fruit and should be separated from the next by the same width as the rectangle width.

Obtain a good length of very thin nylon thread, which can be obtained from a shop selling angling equipment.

Make some holes in your cardboard, knot the thread at one end and thread about half an inch above the first gap. Bring the thread through the rectangle that has been cut out, about one inch top and bottom, and then thread it about one inch from the next rectangular space.

Proceed down the rectangles and up again on the other side. When the whole visual aid has been threaded, the effect will be that the pieces cut out can be raised and lowered and yet still remain part of the visual aid. Move the rectangles down to show words underneath as the talk unfolds.

Presentation

In a number of places in the Bible people are compared to trees (e.g. Ps 1:3, Lk 3:9). Relate Isaiah's words to King Hezekiah concerning the house of Judah, who were told to 'take root downward and bear fruit upward'. Ask how this might apply to a Christian.

(a) *Take root downward*

Some trees can have incredibly deep and strong roots. Paul wrote to the Ephesians and Colossians that they should be rooted in Christ (Eph 3:17, Col 2:6). Reveal *Jesus* in the roots of the visual aid. Why Jesus? Speak about some current views of Jesus which are usually contrary to the biblical picture e.g. weak, superstar. Describe the Jesus of the gospels as tough, strong, courageous, as well as compassionate and loving. Refer to the cross, resurrection and ascension and our need to repent and believe in him. That is how we become rooted in Jesus.

If we have become rooted this should show itself in various ways, which brings us to the second part of our text:

(b) *Bear fruit upward*

The Bible refers to three ways in which we can bear fruit:
° *Fruit of repentance* (Mt 3:8). John the Baptist stressed the need for evidence that repentance was real; that when we confessed our sins, asked God's forgiveness that we really were sorry to God for our sins.
° *Fruit of the Spirit* (Gal 5:22). Is not this the sort of fruit we all want to see around us in the lives of others, as well as ourselves? It can only happen as we receive Jesus and the gift of his Holy Spirit. The evidence that we really have done so is the fruit of the Spirit that other people see in us, just as the fruit all around us at our Harvest Festival is evidence of a lot of planting some time ago.
° *Fruit of souls* Refer to Jn 4:36 and Jesus' explanation that winning people for him was rather like a harvest. Paul in Romans 1:13 explains

how he wanted to win some Roman souls for Christ. It should be the desire and ambition of every genuine Christian to want to win other souls for Jesus.

MICHAEL BOTTING
Editor

40 Sharing—A harvest sermon

TEXT

Mt 25:35–40.

AIM

To demonstrate that our thankfulness for God's gifts must be matched by our willingness to share with those less fortunate.

PREPARATION

You will need a chocolate marshmallow, or something similarly edible: a knife and fork, each attached to the end of a broom handle and, at the other end, some red tape around the handle.

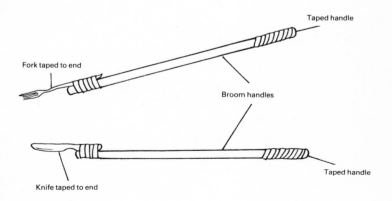

Fork taped to end

Taped handle

Broom handles

Knife taped to end

Taped handle

PRESENTATION

Ask which of the children like marshmallows. Invite one of those who like them to come forward and eat one. There is a condition—they must use the knife and fork, and hold them only by the taped handle. The person will try many ways of getting the marshmallow to his/her mouth, but without success.

Ask the congregation what is needed, and work patiently towards the answer. It needs another person to come, do the cutting, and feed the one who couldn't reach.

A good application is to explain that there is enough food in the world for all to eat, but it needs those who have, to share with those who have not, and this is the duty of the Christian.

BOB METCALF
Liverpool

41 Harvest Sunday

Text

'There is more happiness in giving than in receiving' (Acts 20:35 GNB). This text does not appear in the gospels and the surrounding verses do not make an appropriate reading. Lk 11:5–13 is a suitable reading because it brings out the fact that God loves to give.

Aim

God's purpose is to make us like himself, that is, into people who love to give rather than to get.

Preparation

Make a large card with the word *give* on one side and the word *get* on the other side. You will also need 'labels' for the people in the drama—*God, seed, man* and *Jesus*: these can simply be hung around their necks with pieces of string. Prepare three apples, made of card, and large enough to have the words *love, joy* and *peace* on them. On the other side of the apples you will need a short piece of double-sided tape (or sellotape folded over) to make it easy to stick the apples onto the man. Other props include a watering can, a torch or lamp, and two suitable toys for scene 2.

Presentation

Explain that every time you hold up the large card, the congregation must be ready to shout out the word you hold up—either *give* or *get*. You can give them a bit of a rehearsal: 'Let's make a start and see how we *get* on.' Encourage them to say the word very positively.

Now begin with the following: 'Some people say you've got to *give* as much as you *get* in this life—and most people are just out for what they can *get*. But Jesus said you'll be much happier if you *give* rather than wanting to *get* things for yourself. Indeed, the Bible tells us that the more we *give* the more we will *get* and the more we *get* the more we have to *give*'. Explain that God is one who loves to *give* and lead into scene 1 (see separate script).

After scene 1 explain that because God loves to *give*, he wants us to be people who *give* as well. He wants us to be like him, that's why he made us 'in his image'. Talk about Adam and Eve and say briefly how they spoilt God's plans by sinning...so that now instead of wanting to *give* we just want to *get*. (Scene 2 can then follow without introduction.)

Hands up if that has never happened in your home! Indeed, it's true of every one of us, if we're honest with ourselves. We prefer to *get* rather than *give*...we are selfish, we hold on to what is ours. But does it make us happy?

How then *can* we be happy? God's got the answer! He has given us the greatest gift of all which is the answer to our sin and selfishness. (Straight into scene 3.)

After scene 3, you need to reinforce the point it makes by saying something like: God wants to *give* us his Son Jesus to live within us so that he can produce the best kind of fruit. (Beware of putting in too much 'talk'—the drama should speak for itself.)

Jesus is like the seed and it's God's work (if we allow him) to help that 'seed' to grow in us so that we *can* produce the best kind of fruit and so be more like him. What we have to do is to *give* our hearts to him, so that he can make us into people who love to *give* rather than *get*. Finish with the text (or its equivalent: you'll be much happier if you *give* rather than wanting to *get* things for yourself).

To introduce the text to the congregation earlier in the service, it might be an idea to do a quiz on it—playing 'hang-man' or 'take a letter' is a good way of building up the text which you can then bring back in your talk.

Scene 1

GOD, SEED (a small girl) and MAN.

GOD: Let me give you this (*puts seed in the middle*).

MAN: What is it?

GOD: It's a seed of course.

MAN: What am I supposed to do with it?

GOD: Dig a hole and bury it (*pushes seed down into ground. Seed gives a squeal of protest*).

MAN: That's easy enough. What do I do now?

GOD: Nothing.

MAN: Nothing?

GOD: That's right. I do the rest. I give it water to drink (*takes up watering-can*) and I give it sunshine to help it grow strong and healthy (*takes up cycle lamp and shines it on seed*). Now watch it grow...(*seed stays put*). NOW WATCH IT GROW! (*seed slowly rises up to full height with hands in the air to imitate corn.*)

MAN: That's very clever. But *I* haven't done anything yet.

GOD: I do the difficult bits, you do the easy bits. There's only one thing left to do, and you can do that...cut it down and eat it.

MAN: Oooh thank you! (*Grabs the girl off her feet and walks off with her, to the sound of 'munch, munch'.*)

Scene 2

TWO CHILDREN (played by adults, each with a toy. CHILD 1 is playing with his toy and CHILD 2 is looking on with interest.

CHILD 2: What've you got there? Let me have a look.

CHILD 1: (*turning slightly away*) It's a crane of course—and it's mine so you're *not* having a go with it!

CHILD 2: Oh, go on! Let me just turn the handle and see how it works!

CHILD 1: (*turning away even more and protecting the crane*) No! Go away and let me play on my own. Go and play with your own toys.

CHILD 2: (*angrily*) You're mean that's what *you* are! (*Turns away rather sulkily and begins to play with his own toy*)

CHILD 1: What've you got there? Let me have a look.

CHILD 2:   (*turning slightly away*) It's a cement mixer of course—and it's mine so you're *not* having a go with it!

CHILD 1:   Oh, go on! Let me just turn the handle and see how it works!

CHILD 2:   (*turning away more and protecting the cement mixer*) No! It's mine. Anyway, you didn't let me play with your crane, did you? So why should I give you *my* toys?

CHILD 1:   Well I'm never going to let you play with my toys ever again!

CHILD 2:   And I'm never going to let you play with *my* toys ever again!

BOTH: SO THERE!!
(*They stalk off in opposite directions.*)

Scene 3

GOD, JESUS and the MAN from scene 1

GOD: Let me give you this (*puts Jesus into the middle*)

MAN: Who is it?

GOD: It's my Son of course.

MAN: What do you want me to do?

GOD: Open your heart and receive him into your life. Let him come deep into every part of you (*pushes Jesus gently down into crouching position with the same action as that used for the seed*) like the seed as it goes into the earth.

MAN: What do I do now?

GOD: Let me water that seed that is within you with my Holy Spirit, and let me give it the light of my word (opens Bible over Jesus) to help it grow strong and healthy. Now watch it grow! (*Jesus rises slowly to full height.*)

MAN: It's true—Jesus is growing within me!

GOD: And it's all my work! Now look what Jesus is going to give you as he lives in you: instead of that selfishness and meanness he will give you love* instead of all that unhappiness, he will give you joy*, instead of that worry and anxiety, he will give you peace*; and there's lots more fruit from this seed as well—patience, kindness, goodness, gentleness, faithfulness and self-control.

MAN: Thank you so much—you really have changed me! (*JESUS and the Man walk off together.*)

at this point Jesus sticks the appropriate apple on to the Man.

JOHN CORRIE
Nottingham

42 King Ben-Hadad and King Ahab (Remembrance Sunday)

Text

1 Kings 20.

Aim

To show that we trust and obey God always, including times when things are difficult. Use a blackboard map and get the congregation to follow the story in their Bibles.

Preparation

Draw a map of the Middle East, showing Palestine (Israel), Syria and Assyria. Most good Bibles have maps included or reference might be made to the *New Bible Dictionary* (IVF, edited by J. D. Douglas, 1962); also the three-part *Illustrated Bible Dictionary* (IVP 1980). Have the names *BEN-HADAD* and *AHAB* written conspicuously near where they lived and covered with black card, which can be held onto the board with Sellotape.

Presentation

Make reference to the Second World War and Adolf Hitler, who was a bully and a boaster. He boasted he would rule the world and, like most boasters and bullies, came to a bad end. Ask the children whether they know of boasters and bullies at school. Say that you are going to think of a king who was like that, and ask them to turn in their Bibles to 1 Kings 20. Ask them a number of questions. Who was the king who boasted (vv.1–3)? On receiving the name *BEN-HADAD*, uncover the name on the blackboard. To whom did he boast? Uncover the name *AHAB*, when you receive it. Ask how he picked a quarrel with Ahab (v.3).

Ben-Hadad trusts his army

He tells Ahab his army will carry Samaria away in handfuls. Ahab replies in verse 11, 'Don't boast till you are taking your armour off.' Ben-Hadad takes up his position.

Ahab trusts in God

What will Ahab do? Ask who comes to him (v.13). The prophet explains that the Lord will fight for Ahab. (Read v.14–16). Describe the battle and how Ben-Hadad gets drunk. Ask what happens to the Syrians (v.20–21).

Ben-Hadad listens to bad advice

What happens next to Ben-Hadad (vv.23–25)? Was Ahab prepared for this (v.22)?

Ahab listens to good advice

The prophet told Ahab he would win (v.28). Ask what happened in the battle (vv.29–30), and what happened to Ben-Hadad (vv.31–33). Ask why Ahab allowed this (look at the map). Explain that Ahab wanted Syrian protection from Assyria. Ask why this was absurd— because he had trusted God to save him from Ben-Hadad, surely he could trust him to deliver him from Assyria. Show that God was displeased (vv.42, 43).

Application

'We were thinking earlier about the last war. Many of you do not know what it was like. Like Syria, Germany was very strong. Like Israel, Great Britain was very weak. Germany threatened: we prayed, war was averted. Another threat: war, more prayers, and victory. But how often do we think about God now? How often do we trust and obey God now there is no threat of war? God cannot be very pleased with us if we only go to him in trouble, like Ahab, and forget him when things go well. We should trust and obey him at all times. What about you? Do you trust him when things are difficult?' (End with one or two topical illustrations.)

MICHAEL BOTTING
Editor

43 A poppy (Remembrance Sunday)

TEXT

Jn 15:13.

AIM

To think of those things that we should be remembering this day.

PREPARATION

Cut out four large, leaf-shaped pieces of cardboard (in dark red) to be fixed to a teazlegraph board in the shape of a poppy, with the words *Praise, Offering, Prayer* and *Peace* on them.

Also cut out one small circular piece of card and write *You* on it. (If you can, obtain a copy of the famous *Lord Kitchener needs you* poster from the Imperial War Museum.)

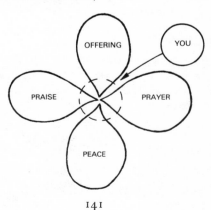

PRESENTATION

Explain the different feelings with which we come to such a service—
from those few people who still have vivid memories of World War 1,
to the young people for whom the world wars are simply history.

What, though, is the one thing that most of us wear and which we
associate with Remembrance Sunday? (A poppy.) Explain the origin
of the poppy (poppies seen growing on the battlefields of the Great
War). Say that you are going to make a large poppy, and that the five
letters P-O-P-P-Y will help us to remember the meaning of this
service.

(a) *Praise* (place first leaf up)

We have come to thank God for his deliverance of our nation in time of
war. Just think what it would have meant if we had been defeated by
Hitler. But sadly, we so soon forget, and so easily take God for
granted.

(b) *Offering* (place second leaf up)

War is not glamorous—millions of people died in the two world wars.
Jesus said: 'Greater love has no man than this, that a man lay down
his life for his friends' (Jn 15:13). (Possibly recount a story from
wartime e.g. from *Miracle on the River Kwai*.) If we are Christians,
though, we stand in the light of the greatest offering ever made—it
was not while we were God's friends, but 'while we were yet sinners
Christ died for us' (Rom 5:8).

(c) *Prayer* (place third leaf up)

We have come to pray for those who have been bereaved as the result
of war, for those who were injured and who still suffer, and for the
leaders of our nation (and all nations) involved in diplomacy. Especially we need to pray for:

(d) *Peace* (place fourth leaf up)

We are not here to glorify war, but to pray for peace—just as the
prophets looked for the time when 'they shall beat their swords into
ploughshares...' (Mic 4:3). This means that we must also pray and

work for a fair and just world. Four leaves—but what holds them together?

(e) *You* (place black circle in the centre)

In the First World War, there was a famous poster of Lord Kitchener pointing his finger to show that your country 'needs YOU' (show it if you have a copy). Other people cannot do your remembering for you—you have to praise God, accept Christ's offering (and offer yourself in return), pray to the Lord, and pray and work for peace in a world which is still being torn apart by war and violence.

PETER BANNISTER
Bridgwater

44 The Victoria Cross and the Victorious Cross (Remembrance Sunday)

TEXT

Jn 3:16, 15:13, and Rom 5:6–11.

AIM

To recall great acts of bravery, sacrifice and rescue by holders of the Victoria Cross, and by Jesus on the Victorious Cross.

PREPARATION

This talk can be presented in one of the following ways:-
1. A large drawing on paper of the Victoria Cross and the Victorious Cross—(present drawing of Victoria Cross first, then present drawing of Victorious Cross).
2. An overhead projector drawing of the Victoria Cross and the Victorious Cross—(reveal drawing of Victoria Cross first and then reveal drawing of Victorious Cross).

PRESENTATION

Today is Remembrance Sunday when we recall the great acts of bravery, sacrifice and rescue achieved by servicemen during two World wars. Can you tell me what medal we have pictured here?

The Victoria Cross

The Victoria Cross is the highest award granted to Commonwealth servicemen for acts of bravery, sacrifice and rescue. War is an evil and we must not seek to glorify war, but in the horror of war the following people showed selfless courage and for this they were awarded the Victoria Cross.

(a) *The youngest V. C. holders*

° *Hospital Apprentice Andrew Fitzgibbon*—a 15 year old boy in the India Medical Establishment who won the V. C. in the Third China War of 1860. Although wounded himself he stayed at his post and continued to help nurse the wounded despite being under heavy fire.

° *Boy John Travers Cornwall R. N.*—A 16 year old boy on the cruiser *Chester* at the Battle of Jutland 1916. He was mortally wounded in the first few minutes of action, but remained standing alone at the exposed gun awaiting orders, his gun crew killed or lying down badly wounded. Cornwall later died from his wounds. He is an example to the Boys Brigade/Life Boys of their motto 'Sure and Steadfast'—even unto death.

(b) *The oldest V. C. holder*

° *Lieutenant William Raynor*, a 69 year old officer in the Bengal Veteran Establishment, who fought in the India Mutiny of 1857. He was defending the ammunition against great odds and he blew up all the ammunition when he realised that defeat was imminent.

(c) *V. C. and Bar holders.*

° *Only three men have won the V. C. twice.* Two of those men never used a gun to gain their awards. Both Captain Noel Chavasse (whose twin brother became a Bishop) and Lieutenant Arthur Martin-Leake were members of the Royal Army Medical Corp. and won their double

V. C.s saving the lives of numerous men in the front line of fire, rescuing the wounded time and time again whilst under heavy fire. The other V. C. and bar holder was New Zealander Captain Charles Upham.

The Victorious Cross

However heroic were the men who won the V. C. medal, the greatest act of bravery, sacrifice and rescue the world has ever known was fought on the battlefield of Calvary.

Enlarge on the victory won at Calvary over Satan and sin, stressing that Jesus not only died for his friends but also for his enemies (Rom 5:6–8) to achieve their forgiveness and freedom.

Notice how many war medals use the word 'cross' in their title— Victoria Cross, Military Cross, Distinguished Flying Cross. In some way they seek to take their standard from the Victorious Cross of Christ, where Jesus showed his love to each of us by his bravery, sacrifice and rescue of fallen mankind.

The former Bishop of Birmingham, Bishop J. L. Wilson, who was a Japanese prisoner of war recommends three thoughts for this Remembrance Sunday:
° Thankfulness for our deliverance and the sacrifice of others.
° Penitence for human sin and evil.
° Dedication to work for peace and justice in the world.

This applies both to the world wars of this century and the cosmic war and the victory of Jesus.

RAY ADAMS
Redditch

45 Dedication festival

TEXT
1 Cor 12:12–13a.

AIM

To show that the Church is people and, though different from each other, all are important.

PREPARATION

Use Lego bricks to make seven-eighths of a model of a church building.

PRESENTATION

Bring the nearly completed Lego building to the beginning of the address. Children can be invited to help the minister to complete it.

Then, using the model point out how in different parts of the building, small bricks and large are needed. Show from the model how wrong it looks if one is not in place.

Then while stripping the model, give this explanation:

Bricks and wood of all shapes and sizes equal peoples.

Mortar and cement equal Spirit, fellowship, prayer

Builder equals God

Foundation stone equals Christ

Windows enable us to look out on the world, and the world to look at us, God's people in order to see God.

BOB METCALF
Liverpool

147

46 Invitation talk

Text
Lk 14:15–24.

Aim

A general gospel talk on some of the excuses people make for refusing God's invitation, based around a fairly elaborate visual aid, together with drama.

Preparation

Construct a large envelope with the following words on the front:
A SINNER,
LOST LANE,
EARTH.
Draw a postmark with *Heaven* on it and *33* AD in the middle. Draw a red stamp with a lamb on it and other marks to suggest the Crucifixion. Mark over the stamp franked wavy lines. Inside the envelope put a card with an invitation:

> *God says*
> *Come to my supper*
> *RSVP*

Make a door out of large piece of cardboard with letter box. Assembly props for drama as mentioned in the presentation. Perhaps you can borrow a postman's uniform and have someone dressed up and hidden from view.

PRESENTATION

Ask who likes going to parties, and make traditional references if it is near Christmas. Explain that you have got an invitation to a party. (The postman appears with the envelope at this point.) Ask to whom it is addressed. Upon receiving the reply, 'A Sinner' ask who that is. Draw out that it means every single one of us on this earth. Because we are sinners we live in 'Lost Lane'.

Ask who the invitation is from. Suggest that a child comes up to see the postmark, which will be too small to be seen at a distance. Explain that this invitation is from God, and that he especially issued the invitation around about 33AD.

Ask someone to suggest what happened then. Draw out the answer that Jesus died. Enquire who pays to send an invitation by post, (answer: 'the sender'). It costs God to send this invitation.

Examine the stamp which has a picture of the Lamb of God, and other symbols suggesting the Crucifixion, explaining briefly what it means. Now produce the invitation from the envelope and read the words on it. Ask what RSVP means. Draw out that we have to reply.

Will everyone want to say 'Yes'? Most people want to go to parties, but the extraordinary thing is, as Jesus pointed out in a story he told most people refuse God's supper for various reasons. Here are some excuses they might give.

Act 1

(Set the scene with a small sofa placed near the lectern. Arrange for two responsible older children to hold up the door with the letter box in it. They move left of stage and as they do so the postman puts a letter through the letterbox.)

Enter First Boy and Girl, (both dressed in jeans, boy carrying saw and wood, girl carrying paint pot and wallpaper). They move to door and girl picks up letter and reads it.

FIRST GIRL: Old money-bags up't mansion wants us to go to have a nosh-up with 'im!

FIRST BOY: What's 'e up to?—Wants to show off 'is new 'ouse, you bet!

FIRST GIRL: Oh Bert—t'would be interesting.

FIRST BOY: O.K. so what! We'll never get this 'ouse done unless we get on with it, and we've got the Jones' coming next week. Yer'd better think of an excuse. (*Both go off*).

Act 2

Children move door to centre and receive another letter from postman.

(Second Boy appears, dressed to go out in a sports car. He picks up the letter and reads.)

SECOND BOY: Samantha, His Lordship wants us to dine with him next Sunday.

SECOND GIRL: (*from gallery or pulpit*) George, we can't, we are driving over to the Lakes then, to try out the new car—you promised!

SECOND BOY: Don't worry darling. I haven't forgotten. I will tell him I must test the car and that is the only day I've got.

Act 3

Children move door to right of stage and receive third letter from postman. Third Boy and Girl appear holding hands. Both are flashily dressed. Boy sits down on sofa and girl picks up letter and looks at envelope.

THIRD GIRL: Mr *and Mrs* Frederick Smith! (*she quickly opens up and reads*). J. B. wants us to go over to his place on the 19th (*pause*)—that will be your first night off since our honeymoon.

THIRD BOY: Don't worry dearest, we'll think of something. Come and sit down. You're not for sharing—not yet anyway! (*They cuddle on the sofa, lights dim*).
(*Children holding door and Third Boy and Girl move off, carrying sofa.*)

End with an appeal for some in the congregation to stop making excuses for not accepting God's invitation to make Christ Saviour and Lord.

MICHAEL BOTTING
Editor

PART THREE
The Christian Life

47 Life's journey

TEXT

Phil 3:20; Eph 2:8–9; Jn 10:10

AIM

To show that we only get to heaven because Jesus made it possible.

PREPARATION

Obtain a poster from British Rail with slogan 'This is the age of the train'. Make a ticket as shown in illustration. You will also need a board and Blu-tack. (The 'trick' could possibly be done with teazlegraph and velcro.)

PRESENTATION

Talk about the different ways in which we can make journeys—car, bus, foot, cycle, train. Refer to slogan 'This is the age of the train' and put up poster. Before you travel on a train you need something. What? A ticket. (Produce your ticket.) Where is it to?

Heaven

When do we begin our journey to heaven? Not when we die, but when we begin the Christian life. Some have a long journey because they become Christians when young, others a short journey because they do not start Christian life until older. The only time we cannot start a journey to heaven is after we have died. Those who have become Christians are citizens of heaven (Phil 3:20). Do I know I am on my way to heaven because I have my ticket? How much is it?

Free

Compare with British Rail prices! Quote Eph 2:8–9. The reason it is a gift to us is that the price was paid nearly 2,000 years ago on the cross. You can't earn it. You need to accept the gift. Have you accepted the gift?

Single

You only go, you do not come back. Story of rich man and Lazarus, (Lk 16:19–31) shows us this. Rich man wanted someone to go from heaven to warn his five brothers about hell, but was told it was not possible. If we are on our way to heaven we will never pass the same point on a return jourey. Mention the date. We will never pass that date again.

First class

Most British Rail adverts are for second class travel. But this journey is not only free, it is first class! Some people don't believe this. They think being a Christian is second class (or third or fourth or twentieth!). They think it is not a good thing at all. Refer to 'life in all its fullness' (Jn 10:10 GNB) as the first class journey we have to heaven. You will find fewer people travel first class.

'The Gospel Train' can be sung as a break here (Youth Praise 144).

You need to keep your ticket in case a ticket collector wants to see it. As yours is a big one you will fold it up. (Fold as indicated in diagram.) Tell the story of one man who did this and someone else tried to steal it. He tore a piece off (tear one piece off), then a second piece (tear second piece). When he arrived at the gate of heaven, he gave in the ticket. (Open out ticket.) But he found it wasn't quite right. (Take pieces one by one and stick them on a board with Blu-tack to spell HELL. So he didn't get into heaven. He then saw original owner of ticket and told him it was no good. But original owner pointed out he had the right half. (Open out other half and stick on board—showing it is a cross.)

Jesus died to pay the price of my ticket to heaven. It is a free, single, first class ticket to heaven. When I get there I have to say to God 'Let

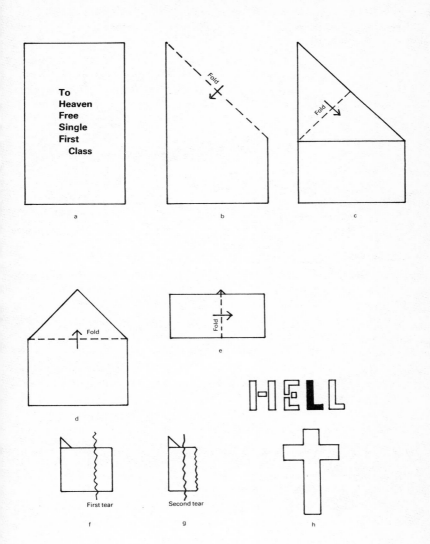

To
Heaven
Free
Single
First
  Class

a

Fold

b

Fold

c

Fold

d

Fold

e

First tear

f

Second tear

g

HELL

h

me into heaven, Jesus paid the price to let me in.' End by asking if they have a ticket. Jesus paid the price. Have they accepted what he did for them?

ALAN PUGMIRE
Manchester

48 The two ways

Deut 30:15.

Aim
To show that we have to choose between God and the Devil.

Preparation
Make a signpost with two arms, one saying *GOOD*, other saying *EVIL*. Make sure there is space for a further letter before the first letter of evil. Prepare a blank card the same size as the letter 'O' in *Good* and a letter 'D' the same size as the letters in *Evil*.

Also prepare two other cards, one saying *LIFE*, the other saying *DEATH*.

Presentation
Ask if anyone has been to camp. Were many people there? Did they walk far to get there? Say you are going to tell the story of a camp with lots of people, who walked 700 miles (from here to... name a suitable place).

One day the leader gathered everyone together because he had something important to say. Tell in modern English (as if Moses were speaking) the story of their journey so far, how they have seen others worshipping other gods. Lead on to text. (Put up your signpost (1).)

Good

Talk about their ideas of being 'good'. Moses saw good as obeying the commandments, loving the Lord and walking the way—the good way.

Evil

People on the journey saw others who worshipped idols. Illustrate from Hopeful in *Pilgrim's Progress* who, when discouraged, hoped he could find an easier path, and was drawn away from God.

Explain there is still a good way and an evil way today. We have to face a decision which road to take.

Life

(Put up sign (2) *life*, either some distance from signpost, in direction of *good*, if you have room, or attach it below *good*.) Refer to Mt 7:13–14 about the road to life being narrow, hard and few on it.

Death

(Put up sign (3) *death* some distance from signpost in direction of *evil*.) Refer to Mt 7:13–14 about road to death being wide, easy and many are on it.

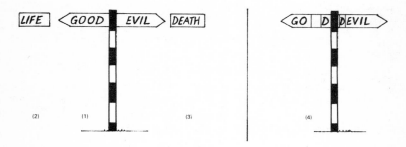

We have to decide which road to take. Talk about destinations to which they lead. (Alter signpost (4) put blank card over 'O' in *GOOD* to make it *GOD*. Put the *D* in front of *EVIL* to make *DEVIL*.) Point out we are in fact choosing between God and the Devil.

ALAN PUGMIRE
Manchester

49 Mr Self and Mr Sinner

Text
Lk 18:9–14.

Aim

To show that a person gets right with God by asking for forgiveness.

Preparation

Gather together some characters from the *Mr Men* series or some books about them. On coloured paper do cut-outs of *Mr Self*, looking important, and *Mr Sinner*, looking down shamefacedly. Do flashcards for the following words: *Mr Self, Mr Sinner, I, VAT, PAYE, Right with God*.

Have a board large enough for all these and have a spire, tower or some characteristic feature of your church to attach to the board. (Teazlegraph or OHP could be used.)

Presentation

Say you have brought some friends along and ask if anyone knows who they are. Talk about the particular *Mr Men* characters you have with you and what is wrong with them. Say you are going to talk about some *Mr Men* about whom no book is written.

(a) (*Put Mr Self and his title on board.*) He was a good man, good at knowing the law. At school he read the school rules and was very careful he didn't do anything wrong. People used to like *Mr Self* because he could tell them how much (or little) they had to do to be good. He was a religious man. He went to church (*put church spiral tower on top of board*). What did he do in church? He prayed. He had a favourite word. It was 'I' (*produce flashcard and fasten to board near him.*) He prayed 'I thank God I am not like Mr—' (refer to some of your original *Mr Men* characters) 'I don't do bad things, like stealing someone else's wife.' Then, when he had told God all the things he didn't do, he told him all the things he did do. 'I fast two days a week' (ask if they know what fasting is), 'I give you one tenth of my income', 'I thank you that I am not like this other man here'. His prayer might have ended with words of Little Jack Horner, 'What a good boy am *I*'. He was concerned about *Mr Self*.

(b) Another man (*put Mr Sinner and flashcard up*) also went to church. He had some favourite words too. (*Produce VAT flashcard.*) What does it mean? (*Produce PAYE flashcard*)—what does it mean? Income tax: *Mr Sinner* was a tax collector. He worked for the Roman government. Tax collectors were cruel then. They took lots of taxes. People didn't care for tax collectors like *Mr Sinner* because when they collected money for the government, they took more for themselves. They did wrong things. But even *Mr Sinner* went to church! He prayed. His prayer: 'God, have pity on me a sinner!'

(c) Ask which one was *Right with God*, (produce flash card). Not *Mr Self* who lived good life. He was a sinner because of his pride. But *Mr Sinner* who admitted his sin, was right with God when he went home. (Put *Right with God* flashcard beside *Mr Sinner*.) Explain that if they want to be right with God it is not by going to church—both men did. It is not by being like *Mr Self*, telling God how good we are, but by being like *Mr Sinner* and telling God how sinful we are–'God, have pity on me, a sinner!' We need to be forgiven. We need to say 'Thank you, Jesus, I can be forgiven. You died for me.' It is something we each need to do. Ask if they have, and whether they will go home 'Right with God'.

ALAN PUGMIRE
Manchester

50 Danish bacon! We must eat to live (or the fried breakfast)

Jn 1:12.

Aim

To show that we only benefit from what God has done for us in Jesus by receiving him into our hearts and lives.

Preparation

Raid the fridge or larder for a slice of bacon, an egg, half slice of bread and a tomato.

You will also need a frying pan, some fat, camping Gas heater or primus, spatula, matches.

Set up the cooking unit in a suitable, safe and visible place.

Also set up a small table—folding card table will do—with a chair, cloth, knife and fork, plate. Again this should be visible.

Presentation

Hands up if hungry...even if only a little bit....

Q1 Come on, who's hungry?   (*Encourage and wait for response*)

What's this?   (*Hold up slice of bacon*)

What else do you have for breakfast?   (*Hold up items you have one by one*)

Well now, we have hungry people, and we have some food; so let's cook it! (*Proceed to cooking unit, light, place rasher in pan and then get any scouts or other suitable persons to take over the cooking.*) While cooking is under way get the people to think of spiritual hunger and its symptoms...longings for peace, purity, joy, happiness, oneness with God...but don't overdo it. *(Keep an eye on the cooking. As cooking nears completion ask next question.)*

Q2 How many think this is good to eat? Do you think it is good? Hands up those who believe it is good?

Q3 Would *you* like to eat it?

Q4 Who will come forward to eat it?

(By now the sizzling hot breakfast should be on the plate on the table. If God has blessed your prayers surrounding this service there should have been decreasing numbers of hands going up for each of the questions, from about three-quarters of full congregation for Q1 to only one or two hands for Q4. Get just one to come forward and eat it then and there before congregation. While the eating takes place, pick up from the earlier thoughts on spiritual hunger.)

God has provided something very wonderful for us.

He knows our souls are hungry.

He has provided everything we need spiritually in Jesus, especially through his death on the cross. But—we must admit our need (our hunger).

How many put up hands if hungry?... Very many of you...Most people have some experience of spiritual hunger.

We must believe that Jesus can meet all our needs—that he died that we might have eternal life. Not so many of you were sure that the breakfast was a good one...fewer hands went up...and not so many people in the world believe that Jesus is the answer to their spiritual needs.

We must take Jesus into our hearts to benefit. How many actually benefited from the breakfast? Just the one who ate it! So just as he (or she) had to take the food into his (or her) mouth to benefit, so we have to take Jesus into our hearts and lives if we want eternal life and our needs met. Sadly, very many fewer people do this—ask Jesus into their hearts and lives.

But what happens if we don't eat food and go on not eating food? We die.

If we don't take Jesus into our hearts and lives we die eternally.

We must eat to live.

We must receive Jesus into our hearts to live eternally and go to heaven.

Note

This was first presented at a service at which there was a visiting group of Danish scouts with a slender grasp of English, hence Danish bacon on that occasion! A dramatic and arresting visual aid was required, with few and simple words.

STEWART SYMONS
Liverpool

51 From hate to love

Jn 3:20; Mt 7:13; Gal 2:20; Mt 10:8 (av); Phil 1:21; 1 Jn 4:19.

Aim

To show the power of Christ to change our lives.

Preparation

Prepare nine cards for children to hold with the following letters *H-A-T-E-G-V-I-L-O*.

Prepare six acetate sheets with the words of the texts given below written on them. Show on OHP at the appropriate moment.

Presentation

Have you ever played the game where you try to change one word into another by altering one letter at a time—and each time you must make up a proper word. We are going to change the word *HATE* into *LOVE*—and this will help us to see what Christ can do for us.

(Ask four children to come up, and give them the cards *H-A-T-E*)

We may not think that we have 'hate' in our life, but this is what the Bible says:

For everyone who does evil hates the light (Jn 3:20)

Explain how all of us have done wrong in God's sight. (Exchange the letter *H* for *G*)

There is a way of changing the direction of our life, though, and the Bible shows that we have a choice to make:

Enter by the narrow gate (Mt 7:13)

Instead of going along with everyone else, on a wide road, there is a small path leading off and a narrow gate through which we can pass (Exchange the letter *T* for *V*)

Just at that place where the narrow road meets the wide road, we can picture the Cross, and underneath are the words:

The Son of God, who loved me and gave himself up for me (Gal 2:20)

Explain the meaning of the cross, and the wonder of Jesus dying in our place there. We cannot earn our salvation, we can only receive it as a gift from the One who gave. Ask the congregation whether they have responded to God's gift in Christ.

Is that the end of it all?

(Exchange the letter *A* for *I*)

No—once we have received God's gift of salvation, we have to give ourselves in service to the Lord and to others. Jesus said:

Freely you have received, freely give (Mt 10:8 AV)

Somebody once said that becoming a Christian is like becoming a member of a club in which the joining fee is nothing, but the annual subscription is everything you've got! The missionary Jim Elliott (killed by the Auca Indians) wrote, 'He is no fool who gives what he cannot keep to gain what he cannot lose.' How much are we giving?

(Exchange the letter *G* for *L*)

Behind all this is the need to have Christ at the very centre of our life. Paul wrote:

For me to live is Christ (Phil 1:21)

Real life is only found in him. Do we know that Christ is controlling what we think and say and do? Only in this way can we complete our word change.

(Exchange the letter *I* for *O*)

The Bible says:

We love because he first loved us (1 Jn 4:19)

Jesus took the first step, and Jesus is the One who can change the attitude of our hearts. Thank God that he can change *Hate* into *Love*!

PETER BANNISTER
Bridgwater

52 Deep trouble!

TEXT

1 Jn 1:8, 9.

AIM

To teach that we need to be opened up to be really mended.

PREPARATION

It is best to time this to coincide with major sewer repairs in your neighbourhood—the impact is then so much more relevant and the parable more meaningful. This was prepared with OHP as two separate pictures, but can be adapted for card, and more than two pictures, by subdividing if desired.

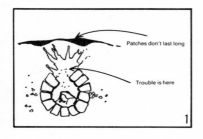

PRESENTATION

Coronation Street has been in an unsatisfactory state for many years. Overnight dips appear...even large holes. Men come and fill them,

167

but the road is still very bumpy and it isn't long before more patches are required. So now we have 'Road closed' and 'Men at work' signs up and they are digging right down to the deep trouble. (Show picture 1).

The deep trouble is a faulty sewage disposal system. Bricks in the old system are caving in.

This is a parable. We are like roads. We develop faults and bumpy surfaces....

We grow bad tempered and irritable.

We let people down and give them a rough ride....

We make life difficult for parents and other people....

We are not very popular.

At first we try patching things up. Parents try to help with a bit of discipline perhaps. Teachers at school try to show the right way forward. We try turning over a new leaf with new resolutions. But it doesn't really work. Sooner or later we need a major rebuild. All of us! The trouble is deep down with the sin disposal system.

So (show picture 2)...

We must put up 'Road closed' signs. There are things to be renounced. And we must put up 'Men at work' signs.

DIY goodness doesn't work in the long run and won't get us right for heaven. We need to call in Christ, the major contractor, who repairs us at his own expense.

Quote 1 Jn 1:8, 9 to close.

STEWART SYMONS
Liverpool

53 Growing on from baptism

TEXT

'Continue to grow in the grace and knowledge of our Lord and Saviour Jesus Christ' (2 Pet 3:18 GNB)

AIM

To help parents, godparents, and others to realise what is necessary if children, and we ourselves, are to grow spiritually as well as physically.

PREPARATION

You will need:

(1) Either a pot plant or a flower pot and a bulb ready for planting.

(2) The words—*Light, Water* and *Warmth* ready to put up on a board.

(3) Three drawings to show what happens if a plant lacks one of these. (These drawings can be done with colour on white card or an overhead projector.)

PRESENTATION

(a) *Remind the congregation: That when a child is born it needs feeding* if it is to grow—(this can be elaborated upon with some extra visual aid, e.g. a baby's bottle, if desired).

That baptism symbolizes spiritual birth (refer to words of baptism service). Children need to grow spiritually (refer to text above) so do we all. For spiritual growth we need spiritual food.

(b) *Illustration*: show pot plant. Ask 'What three things does it need to grow properly?'

The answers are—*Light, Water* and *Warmth*. Put up these words as you receive the answers. All three are essential. (Fertiliser is *not* essential.)

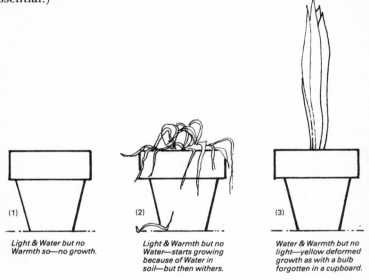

(1)

Light & Water but no Warmth so—no growth.

(2)

Light & Warmth but no Water—starts growing because of Water in soil—but then withers.

(3)

Water & Warmth but no light—yellow deformed growth as with a bulb forgotten in a cupboard.

Show drawings (1), (2), (3) to illustrate what happens if one is missing.

(c) *Application:* A child needs the same three things to grow spiritually: *Light, Water* and *Warmth*—indeed we all need them.

Light (point to the word)

Ps 119:105 says about God's word 'Your word is a lamp to guide me and a light for my path' (GNB) Expand on the need to teach Bible stories to children, and to encourage them to read the Bible on their own, setting an example by your own Bible reading.

Water

The Lord Jesus said (Jn 7:37) 'Whoever is thirsty should come to me and drink.' We must turn to Jesus in prayer for our spiritual needs. We need to teach our children to pray, at first praying with them. We need to pray ourselves, as Jesus often encouraged his followers to do.

Warmth

The early Christians realised the importance of meeting together to worship God and to help each other (expand on this from Acts 2:42–47). We need to do the same on Sundays and at other times, and we need to bring our children with us to do so from an early age.

We need *all three* of these things so that we can grow properly— light, water and warmth—refer back to the pictures briefly as you teach what follows.

° If we read our Bibles and pray (*Light* and *Water*), we miss out on the warmth of worship and meeting with other Christians.

° If we just come to Church and read our Bibles (*Warmth* and *Light*), we miss out on what God wants to give us in answer to our prayers.

° If we just pray and come to church (*Water* and *Warmth*), we do not learn what God wants to teach us through his written word.

The *LIGHT* of God's word, the *WATER* of God's answer to our prayers, and the *WARMTH* of worship and fellowship—you and your child need all three of them to grow spiritually, and so do I.

EDWARD PRATT
Southsea

54 Baptism

TEXT

Mk 1:6–8.

AIM

To show that we try to be good for God, but that we cannot do so in our own strength.

PREPARATION

You will need a glass of water, a clean white handkerchief, a small bottle of tincture of iodine, a plain cross, a second glass containing a solution of sodium thiosulphate (photographic fixer).

Prepare by placing both glasses on a table and the cross lying flat behind the glass containing the fixer solution.

PRESENTATION

(a) Ask the children if they are always good! When they are eventually honest, ask what sort of naughty things they do. (For each answer splash a little iodine on the corner of the handkerchief.)

Then ask the adults if they ever do anything wrong. Things which are wrong and hurt other people or God, are then described as sin. (As before, splash iodine on the handkerchief.)

(b) We really want to be good people for God and for each other, so we try to make ourselves better. (Wash the now brown corner of the handkerchief in the glass of water. The handkerchief will go black and the water will go brown.) Explain that the more we try by ourselves

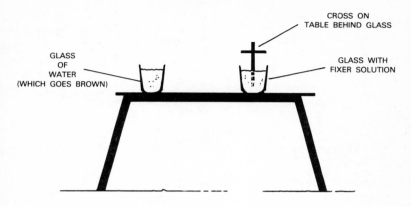

the worse mess we get into. (Remove the handkerchief from the water.) The effect of the brown water is the effect we have on other people—making them miserable and unhappy.

(c) Jesus baptised with water and the Holy Spirit. (Lift the cross—symbolizing Jesus—from behind the second glass.) Explain that we must take our sinfulness and naughtiness to God in prayer and worship, in Bible-reading and fellowship. This second glass is the water of baptism. (Dip the black corner of the handkerchief in this water containing the fixer solution) and the handkerchief will go white again, the liquid remaining clear.

(d) Now for the effect of the Christian on other people. (Without wringing out the handkerchief, dip it into the other glass where the water went brown. The water will immediately clear.) Talk of making other people happy because of our Christian belief and practice.

BOB METCALF
Liverpool

55 Worship

Text
Col 3:16, 17.

Aim

To teach that true worship can only ascend to God as the fire of the Holy Spirit burns brightly within us.

Preparation

This is for presentation with the OHP Flipatron system in which one sheet is superimposed on another—in this case there are six. Prepare each carefully so that, superimposed, all six make the complete picture. Use different colours, such as red for wording on the left, and blue on the right; and appropriate colours for pan, logs, fire etc. As each pair of logs is added additional glow can be added to the fire.

PRESENTATION

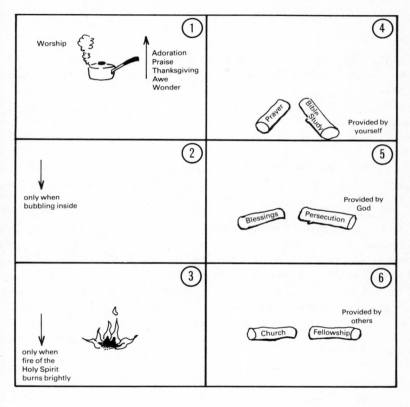

STEWART SYMONS
Liverpool

56 Work, rest and worship

Text
Mk 6:30–46.

Aim
To teach the proper stewardship of time.

Preparation

Design visuals for the teazlegraph board, each backed with velcro, of a clock face, calendar, and a circular disc with each quarter a different colour to represent the seasons, such as green for spring, yellow for summer, buff for autumn and white for winter. Also have visuals to represent *work*, such as a spade or fork, *rest,* such as a bat and ball or a gramophone record and *worship*, such as figures with uplifted arms, an open Bible and praying hands. The three nouns that form the title of this talk should be on strips of teazle-covered card.

Presentation

You are thinking about a very strange thing. We all have been promised just so much, but some will have more, others less. All of us will use up the same amount by the end of this service. Here are some illustrations of it. (Put up clock face, calendar and seasons disc.) By now someone should have mentioned 'time'.

Go on to say that God has made us responsible as to how we use it and ask what should be included in our use of time. Mention with texts, sleeping (Ps 3:5), working (Gen 2:15), eating (Gen 2:16), exercising (1 Tim 4:8), worshipping (Lk 4:16) and resting (Mk 6:31).

God intended us especially to do these things. (Put up visuals alongside three main words as you proceed with the talk.)

Work (Mk 6:31b)

God is a worker and made us in his image. Jesus was a carpenter and preacher. Paul was a tent-maker and taught the importance of work. Work is one of the ways in which we can serve and glorify God, quite apart from bringing us pay and often much pleasure. Because of sin, however, much work is hard. Refer to the problem of unemployment, which the Bible sees as a sign of God's judgment (Zech 8:10). Jesus' parable of the labourers in the vineyard suggests there has always been unemployment, and probably always will be till he returns. Out of work Christians should be encouraged to be involved in voluntary work, of which there is an enormous amount to be done.

Rest (Mk 6:31a)

God has worked into our lives proper time for rest. Refer to the clock, calendar and seasons disc and explain about the need to rest each day, take a day off each week and a holiday in the year, perhaps explaining how even the earth rests through the pattern of the seasons. Reference can be made to the failure of the French experiment to get more work out of people by trying a ten day week. Mention the folly of working seven days a week and doing homework on Sundays.

Worship (Lk 4:16, Mk 6:46)

The Sabbath was also designed for worship and God obviously intends that we should include it in our use of time, mainly in two ways:
° weekly together as we are now
° daily in private Bible reading and prayer.

Conclude by telling the well-known story, perhaps apocryphal, of Henry Ford helping a driver of one of his cars. He designed the car, so knew how it worked best. The Bible is God's handbook for human maintenance, which should include work, rest and worship.

Eddy Stride, Rector of Spitalfields in East London, tells of a boy who had tatooed on his shoulders *Death before employment*. 'Anyone who works is a nut!' he said. Later, out of sheer boredom, he got work in a pre-cast concrete factory and was thrilled by it. God knows best.

Do our lives have a right balance of work, rest and worship?

MICHAEL BOTTING
Editor

57 The body of Christ—the church

1 Cor 12:12–26.

AIM

That members of the congregation shall realise how important each one is, if the local church is to function properly.

PREPARATION

Make a figure from stiff paper or card with separate limbs i.e. head, two ears, trunk, two arms, two hands with one detachable thumb, two legs, two feet with one detachable toe and one 'sore' toe.

All parts except the head to be reversed during the talk and written on.

Means of attaching both sides of the visual aid to the board need to be devised. (Velcro on teazlegraph board is ideal.)

Have pencils or wax crayons and table available for use during the talk.

Have the body assembled on the board but covered before the talk starts.

PRESENTATION

Ask, 'What is the Church?' discuss the answers and bring out that the Church is people who love Jesus, meet to worship and belong together.

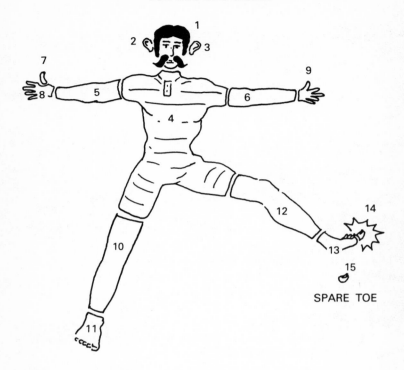

SPARE TOE

Body (Uncover visual of body)

What is this? What shall we call him? (Get suggestions e.g. Fred.) Like most of us Fred has—how many hands? toes? ears…. What is the most important part of Fred? His head? (Remove head) Is the head Fred? Is the body without the head Fred? What makes Fred Fred? (All of him.)

If he had an accident and lost a hand (remove hand) is he still Fred? If he lost a thumb (remove thumb) what difference would it make? (Get the children to pretend to have no thumb and try to pick up a book.) If he stubbed his toe (replace normal toe with sore toe) how would he feel? Bring out the point that if a small part of us hurts it affects the whole of us.

Local church

In 1 Cor 12 the Church is said to be like a body. The Holy Spirit makes us members of the body/Church and unites us to one another like the nerves or blood in a body (v.13). All the parts are different, but all are important and need each other. Bring out the teaching from vv.14–21. The body is controlled by the head who is Jesus (Eph 4:15).

Ask for twelve volunteers from among children. Give each a limb from the body, except the head, and ask them to write their names clearly on the reverse side. Have a table and some help at hand. Then reassemble the body with the names showing.

Get everyone in the congregation to imagine their name is written on one part. If your part is missing or not working or growing properly, what happens? (Remove arm.) Or if your part tries to be another part e.g. hand tries to be foot, what happens? The body is incomplete, it cannot work properly and other parts are upset. (Replace arm.) Bring out the point that we all need to do our part well and have no need to be jealous of others.

Application—it is important for

(a) *The church to grow and be effective.* A healthy church will have as members, people with different gifts, backgrounds, ages, outlooks, working together in the power of the Spirit.

(b) *The individual to belong and have a contribution to make.* There should be mutual caring (v.25). As in a body when a tooth aches or toes are cold, the whole body is affected and takes action, so it is in the local church (v.26).

It is a tremendous privilege to belong to the body of Christ. We are there by courtesy of the Holy Spirit, responsible to the Head and to the rest of the body, in order that the church can grow and be effective.

JUDITH ROSE
Bradford

58 Listening for God

TEXT

Ps 46:10; Jn 20:19–23.

AIM

To let the children know that we have to listen as well as to talk, both with God and with each other. It makes the point that the brain is the finest computer invented—and by God.

PREPARATION

A number of sound effects can be recorded on to a tape e.g. train
  thunder
  bird-song
  knocking on a window
  sea-wash
Following these a number of theme tunes from well-known programmes can also be recorded onto the tape.

PRESENTATION

(a) As a sort of quiz, play the sound effects asking the audience if they can recognise them.

(b) Making this a little harder, play the theme tunes, similarly asking for recognition. Add the comment that the children and adults are using their own computer, their brains, which work as fast as the answers come.

(c) Prayer is listening to God and letting him feed his information into our brain computer so that the answer comes out as to how we should serve him.

(d) Ask an adult to read the second passage, about the Easter Day story. Make the point that the disciples listened to Jesus, and that he gave them a message to proclaim and a job to do—whisper a message to one person only. Then ask that person to pass the message on, whispering to the next person and so on until without your saying anything, the message gets around the church because everyone had to listen.

BOB METCALF
Liverpool

59 Prayer

Text

Mt 7:7.

Aim

To teach some basic facts about prayer.

Preparation

You need cardboard for words and the help of four children to hold words in front of the congregation.

Begin with a picture of a girl, *ALISON SARAH KING* or any boy or girl whose initial letters are A-S-K. (Best of all if you have someone in your congregation.) You will need a board to display words. A teazlegraph cloth was used when this talk was given, to which cardboard was attached with the words on it.

The board should have on it the words ASK, SEEK, KNOCK. You will need to cut out these letters, or write in thick felt marker. The initial letters A-S-K in *Ask, Seek, Knock* should be in a different colour to make them stand out.

Three children hold up cards in turn which read *GOOD THINGS, GOD'S WILL, FORGIVENESS* on the front, and on the back (in the same order) *THE LOST, THE LORD, HALLELUJAH*.

Finally, you will need the words *Knock and it shall be opened* on a larger separate card. If you are fortunate enough to have a door leading on to a platform in front of the congregation, the person who has this card can be hidden behind the door which he opens when someone knocks on it at the end of the talk.

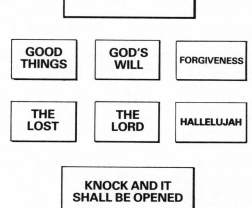

PRESENTATION

We have a new member in our congregation today. (Put up picture of girl, smiling.) She loves choruses. Her name is *Alison Sarah King*. Put up the word *ASK* on the board in two ways:

A   S   K
S
K

The Bible tells us to *ASK* because it shall be given to us, but what shall we ask for?

First child brings up card with *GOOD THINGS*. Give examples of good things, e.g. wisdom of Solomon. Give an example of bad things to contrast.

Second child brings up a card with *GOD'S WILL*. Give example of Jesus praying not for his will but his Father's will to be done before he went to the cross.

Third child brings up the card with *FORGIVENESS* on it. Here quote the Lord's prayer and the story of the Prodigal Son as examples.

Put up the second word *SEEK* and as the second letter of *A-S-K* is the S you need only add the letters *EEK*. The three children now turn over their cards to reveal words which show who God seeks and who we must seek.

° The first child has *THE LOST*. Explain how Jesus has come to seek and save those who are lost. The lost sheep is an example.

° The second child has *THE LORD*. Make the point that we come to seek the Lord. Give an example of someone who has found the Lord by seeking him and perhaps use the words 'Seek the Lord while he may be found, call upon him while he is near.'

° The third child has the word *HALLELUJAH*. Explain that we must all seek to praise God for his goodness to us.

Now return to the board and add the letters: *NOCK* to the K of *ASK*. This part of the talk will have to be adapted according to the building you are in. If you have a platform with a door leading off place someone behind the door, out of sight of the congregation, holding a text on a card which reads 'Knock and it shall be opened unto you'.

The selected child goes to the door and knocks. The person behind the door opens it and walks in revealing the words on the card.

In a building where the door is not in front of the congregation you will have to find some other way of revealing the text with a knock.

At this point explain how God has promised to answer our requests and reveal his will to us. Some may want to use Rev 3:20: 'Behold, I stand at the door and knock, if any man hears my voice and opens the door, I will come in to him and eat with him, and he with me.' Describe the picture by Holman Hunt which hangs in St. Paul's Cathedral, London which is based on this verse. End with Mt 7:7.

CHRISTOPHER PORTEUS
Beckenham

60 Temptation

TEXT

1 Cor 10:13b. (The Greek word used here for 'way of escape' means 'a mountain pass'.)

AIM

To teach that God will always provide a way through our difficulties.

PREPARATION

On a large board (possibly teazlegraph, or the whole talk could be adapted for the overhead projector) have a black triangle, representing a road vanishing into the distance. Prepare cardboard cacti, etc., to be stuck on the board by the roadside, and a series of horizons. The horizons should represent an impenetrable range of mountains, coming successively closer. (See below.)

PRESENTATION

Start with just the road and distant horizon on the board (1). It will not be recognizable.

Describe a journey across a great flat desert in a car. Hold up the cacti, etc. What are they? Place them on the board: the picture starts to emerge (2).

Describe the progress of the journey: sun, heat, hours of driving, as you speak put up successive horizons (more than the series of four shown here may be used (3)).

As the mountains begin to loom, what will happen? There seems to be no way round. They are too high to climb over (4).

Just as it seems that the road will peter out the pass is seen. Remove distant cacti and put up final horizon (5). A way through! The city is a few miles further on.

In life we go through hard times: temptation, hardship, despair, financial worries. God is faithful and will always provide the way through, if we are faithful to him.

STEVEN FOSTER
Redditch

61 Red alert—the secrets of Christian victory

AIM

To show that the Bible offers us victory through Christ, over the spiritual forces of evil.

PREPARATION

This talk, when originally given in St George's Hall, Bradford at the Northern Pathfinder and CYFA Rally in 1973, followed a very vivid dramatic presentation of the forces of evil being overcome through the power of Christ. It was illustrated by suitable pictures on an overhead projector. Anyone using this talk outline should therefore obtain the services of a good artist who can illustrate the talk as liberally as possible.

PRESENTATION

(a) We are all engaged in a real battle, because this wonderful world which God has made for us to enjoy has been invaded by an evil power totally opposed to God and anything good. It all began in heaven when Satan dared to make himself like the Most High God. Then Satan lied to Eve and made her think that God was keeping something back from her. So she fell into sin and Adam, her husband did too.

(b) When God sent Jesus into the world to save us from our sins, Satan tried to get rid of him. Refer to the slaying of the innocents at the first Christmas, his temptations in the wilderness and the Garden of

Gethsemane. However Jesus did not avoid going to the cross, where he died for our sins and cried from the cross the great word of victory *IT IS FINISHED*. He was totally victorious over the powers of evil and Satan was vanquished. The following resurrection and ascension were all part of the evidence.

(c) Although Satan is ultimately beaten, yet he is still around fighting a last ditch stand and doing his best to disrupt this world and prevent men and women, boys and girls following Jesus. War, famine, crime, mugging, ouija boards, are all evidence that Satan is still alive and well and living on planet earth.

BEWARE! You and I are not going to take much notice of Satan all the time we think of him as a big joke—someone who runs around in pink tights, has horns and carries a three-pronged fork. Deception is his business, and he is no better pleased than when he convinces people he does not exist. He lied to Eve and he will to us, especially by suggesting that God is keeping good things back from us and that the path to life can be found through drink, drugs, sex and the occult.

Satan also sows big doubts about Jesus. Should we fall into sin, though he is the tempter, he will jeer at us and say 'Call yourself a Christian and you behave like that!' He is very fond of appearing like a roaring lion, so that we are scared to stand up for Jesus as Peter was when his master was arrested. Actually a lion is least dangerous when it roars; it is the hunting lion that is quiet.

What are the secrets of victory?

° *We must be on the victory side*. Tell the story of the Frenchman who became a naturalised Englishman. When asked what difference it made he replied that whereas previously he had lost the Battle of Waterloo, now he had won it! When we join Jesus' side, we enter into his victory.

° *We must live the victory life*. Enlarge on the need to put self on the cross. (See *The Message of Galatians* by John R. W. Stott, IVP, pp.150–2, for a particularly helpful treatment of this subject). Then deal with the need for Bible reading, prayer, the Church, worship, witness and the power of the Holy Spirit. End with promise in Rev 3:21.

MICHAEL BOTTING
Editor

62 Think no evil

TEXT

Mt 5:21–28.

AIM

To teach that evil thoughts are just as sinful in God's eyes as evil actions and one can easily lead to the other.

PREPARATION

Using long strips of velcro (which can always be used later for other teazlegraph talks) make an outline of an iceberg on the teazlegraph board. Only about a seventh is showing above light blue velcro representing the sea surface.

Have the words *MURDER* and *ADULTERY* on strips of card covered with teazle material.

Using different coloured day-glo card draw four pictures representing *hate* (red card with a dagger), *anger* (orange card with a springing tiger), *envy* (green card with weeds) and *lust* (pink card with semi-clad figure). The four words can be worked into pictures.

Have the word *SIN* on a piece of card, and a red cross to go across it; a flame to represent the Holy Spirit and a face with lines on the forehead to suggest thought. Each should be backed with velcro.

PRESENTATION

(Show the outline of the iceberg and ask for ideas of what it might be. Ascertain that only a small proportion of the iceberg is visible above the surface of the sea.) Today we are going to think about two of God's commandments: not to murder or commit adultery. (Place the two words above the sea surface.)

Murder means to deliberately kill for personal gain. Adultery is an umbrella term for any misuse of our sexual instincts, whether it be sex before marriage or wife swopping after it. Now if you were asked how many here had broken either of these commandments probably no one would own up, because probably no one literally had. Does that mean there is nothing more to say? However if you were asked how many of you had thought about either....? We say 'If looks could kill...' or 'I wish you were dead.' That is why we are calling this talk 'Think no evil'.

Now ask why we have an iceberg on the board, and draw out that thoughts are invisible below the surface, but do occasionally appear in actions. Evil thoughts can lead to evil actions. For instance:

(a) *Hate* (Put *hate* visual in iceberg under sea surface). Refer to the hatred of the religious leaders in Jesus's day which led to murder. Religious people have at times put one another to death, for instance during the Reformation and in Ireland today. Nursing hate can ruin our lives and if we cannot forgive someone then God says he cannot forgive us.

(b) *Anger* (Read Mt 5:22.) Explain how a tiger suddenly pounces. Cain killed Abel because of anger. Jesus tells us we must make up our quarrels quickly, and Paul says that the sun should never set on our wrath.

(c) *Envy* was responsible for the worst crime in history (Mt 27:18). This sin can be rather like a weed that keeps coming up despite uprooting, smothering, poisoning. It works underground and then suddenly comes to the surface in a disgraceful word, letter or action. We can be envious of people's possessions, job, gifts, homes, skill at games, even their apparent success in Christian work. Envy can grow in us all: children, housewives, school-teachers, doctors, even ministers of religion!

(d) *Lust* (Read Mt 5:27–8.) Make it clear this can have nothing to do with enjoying the sight of a pretty girl or handsome man, or else no marriage would ever be a love match (not of the romantic kind, anyway). Jesus is quite clear that this refers to allowing the mind to dwell on impure thoughts, which can lead to the misuse of sex.

This will mean that we must be careful what books we read, films or TV plays we watch. Perhaps mention the story of David and Bathsheba, and that horrific murders have arisen through the reading of pornography. The Bible teaches that the only right use of sex is in the context of marriage. God invented it and planned it for our good.

How do we deal with evil thoughts that can lead to evil actions?

° Confess as soon as we fall into sinful thought. Refer to texts like Prov 28:13, Ps 32:1–5, the stories of David and Bathsheba or the woman taken in adultery. Put up the visual of *SIN* covered by the cross.

° Ask the Holy Spirit to help us set our minds upon him (Rom 8:5ff.). Put up visual of the flame.

° Point out the need for positive and pure thinking (Phil 4:8). Put up visual of the face.

Think about these things.

MICHAEL BOTTING
Editor

63 Don't worry!

TEXT

Mt 6:25–34.

AIM

To teach members of the family of any age the futility of being anxious.

PREPARATION

Use the teazlegraph board and prepare strips to be placed on it with the following words *worry is, senseless, needless, faithless*. Also have some simple cut-outs with velcro on the back of a bird, flower, some food and clothes.

PRESENTATION

Whatever age we are we can be tempted to worry: school, exams, games, illness, unemployment, the children, money, clothes, food, a house, death…the list is endless. If you do not believe in God and have never committed your life to Jesus Christ, then there is nothing more to be said. Life is meaningless and you are a puppet in the hand of blind chance. You have good reason to worry, I would!

But if you really are a Christian, then Jesus has a very clear message for you: 'Don't worry'. In our lesson (assuming it has been read during the Family Service) Jesus says five times we should not be anxious, that is we should not worry, and gives three reasons why we shouldn't. (Put up at the top of the teazlegraph board *worry is*: then on the left-hand side put the other three words as you come to speak about them.

Worry is senseless (v.25)

God gave us bodies and life; we could do nothing about that so surely we can trust him to feed and clothe us (v.26). Jesus says 'Your heavenly Father feeds them', i.e. the birds who cannot call God their Father. If he looks after them, how much more we can be sure he will look after us. Put up the bird opposite the word senseless (v.27). We cannot lengthen our span of life, but worry might well shorten it.

Worry is needless (vv.28–30)

God clothes the lily, or any flower for that matter, which only lasts for a short while, yet so magnificently as to outshine the glory of Solomon, so surely he can and will look after us who are his children. (Put up the flower opposite the word needless.)

Worry is faithless (vv.30–33)

Stress 'men of little faith'. To be constantly worried about food, drink and clothes shows lack of faith in our heavenly Father. This is not saying that these things do not matter, but they should not totally absorb us. To do so is to behave like Gentiles, that is, like those who do not believe. All around us there are lots of people in this parish (or area) whose lives are dominated by food and drink and clothes. (Put up pictures on board opposite the word faithless.) But we Christians have a far greater and important concern, the kingdom of God.

End with a story of someone who really did exercise wonderful faith and God so obviously provided for his or her needs. Gladys Aylward or former 'Wiretapper' Jim Vaus are especially good examples. Perhaps some of you here are thinking 'Oh, but things just don't happen in my life like that.' Have you ever given God a chance? Let us do so now. Let us bow our heads for prayer.

MICHAEL BOTTING
Editor

64 Cheer up!

TEXT

Mt 9:1–7.

AIM

To teach that the surest way to real happiness is by receiving the Gospel.

PREPARATION

This talk was originally shown on Yorkshire Television in 1974. An artist in the congregation painted three pictures illustrating the text—four men carrying the sick man on a stretcher, Jesus leaning over the sick man, and the man standing upright holding his stretcher and looking radiantly happy. I also had the words on teazle-covered strips of card *forgiveness*, *freedom*, and *faith* and the word *sin* with a red day-glo cross to go across it, two heart shapes in red and pink day-glo card and two flame shapes in red and orange day-glo card. The hearts and flames were fixed together in pairs so that part of the pairs could be seen behind the other. All the visuals had velcro stuck on the back.

PRESENTATION

Ask how people are feeling today. Suggest problems that may be making them worried or unhappy. You could hardly be worse off than the man we heard about in the reading (assuming it had been read as the Lesson in the Family Service). He was paralysed with no National Health Service or social security. Put up on left-hand side of teazlegraph board the picture of the men carrying the stretcher and under it the man lying on the ground with Jesus looking over him.

When friends of the sick man brought him to Jesus he said to him 'Take heart' or 'cheer up'. (These words could also be put at the top of the board if there is room.) Ask 'So what?' Explain that Jesus went to the heart of the problem, which was *sin*. Put the word on the right-hand side of the board at the same level as the lower picture. Jesus said 'Your sins are forgiven'. Some people might think he was missing the point. But things have not changed. The cause of the world's problems, and yours and mine individually, is the human heart, out of which, said Jesus, come evil thoughts, theft, murder, adultery, coveting. What then is Jesus' remedy for cheering us up?

Forgiveness (Put up the word between the second picture and the word *sin*.)

What right had Jesus to offer the sick man forgiveness, the religious leaders quite rightly asked, since God is the only one who can forgive sin? Explain that when we sin we often hurt other people, but supremely God. David quite rightly admitted in Ps 51 after sinning over Bathsheba and Uriah the Hittite that it was against God that he had sinned. But how can God forgive when he has expressly said, the soul that sins must die? The answer lies in Jesus.

Enlarge on his primarily coming to earth to be the Saviour of mankind, mentioning the name he was given at his birth, and the cancelling of sin on the cross on the first Good Friday. (Place the red cross across the word *sin* on the board.) The evidence that Jesus had the right to tell the man his sins were forgiven was that he had the power to make him get up and walk.

Freedom (Put up the third picture under the second and the word *freedom* alongside.)

Just as Jesus was able to free the man from his sickness so he could free him and us from sin. He did this by sending us his Holy Spirit, after ascending to his Father in heaven. (Put up the tongues of fire alongside *freedom*.) Ask what this really means? Not freedom to do as I like, but freedom to do what I should. Perhaps illustrate with a graphic story of someone freed from sin through Christ.

Faith

Perhaps you are saying that forgiveness and freedom are just what you want, but want to know how to get it. Refer to the four men that brought the sick man to Jesus. It was when Jesus saw their faith that he was able to act. (Put up *faith* opposite the top picture and the two hearts on the right-hand side of the board.) Explain faith in terms of trust and exhort congregation to cheer up.

Michael Botting
Editor

PART FOUR

Biblical Characters and Miscellaneous Talks

65 Joshua and his house

Josh 24:15.

AIM

Life is made of making the right decisions. The story of Joshua sets a valuable example.

PREPARATION

If possible show the film-strip *Joshua, Captain of the Lord's Hosts* (produced by Concordia Cat. No.448) with a very vivid recorded sound track, using voices from the congregation and plenty of sound effects.

PRESENTATION

Life is made up of choosing: sweets, toys, TV, friends. And as we get older: job, house, life-partner. Explain to the children that increasingly your parents should be expecting you to make your own decisions. Refer to the text and Joshua's example in decision making. Ask what is the most important decision in life that we can make. Draw out from the text:

(a) *Which God?*

The children of Israel had gathered together at Shechem (Josh 24:1). This was the very place where many years before the patriarch Jacob buried the idols in his house under an oak, and built an altar to the

Lord. Joshua gave the children of Israel three choices: the gods before they came to Canaan, the gods after they came to Canaan or the true God, the Lord. Why should they choose the Lord? Joshua outlined all that the Lord had done, as we heard in the sound-strip such as the taking of Jericho and Ai.

What about ourselves? What are our idols? Refer to such things as money, cars, TV, sex, pleasure, the occult. Ask what the Lord has done that we should choose him? Refer to the cross, the resurrection, the gift of the Holy Spirit, the provision of the Church and sacraments. Explain that the Lord does not just want our outward worship: church attendance on Sunday, a tip in the collection box, the visit on the special occasion like a baptism, wedding, carol service or a funeral. He wants our whole lives. Joshua said, 'Choose…whom you will….' What?

(b) *Serve*

To serve means to turn from other gods and obey the Lord. This is because of two facts we know about the Lord (v.19).
° He is holy.
° He is jealous.

Explain both terms. Joshua had to warn the people about being fickle. The Lord only wants those who will rise to the real challenge. An army is as strong as its weakest man. Reference can be made to Christ's challenge to discipleship and the need to count the cost (Lk 14:25–33), also to the baptism service decision questions: Do you turn to Christ? Do you repent of your sins? Do you renounce evil?

(c) *Me and my house*

Like any good leader, Joshua was not asking of the children of Israel anything he was not prepared to do himself 'As for *me and my house*, we will serve the Lord.' Refer to the solidarity of the family in the Bible as illustrated by Abraham, Isaac, the Philippian jailer. Do you see your family as God's basic unit?

Ask when Joshua expected the people to make up their minds?

(d) *Today*

'Seek the Lord while he may be found', 'Now is the day of Salvation'

202

say the Scriptures. Refer to the typical commercial advert: 'You cannot live without 'SPLOSH' in your home. Get some TODAY.' The devil is always saying there is plenty of time to make up your mind about the Lord. The Holy Spirit is saying you should make up your mind TODAY.

End by explaining how, if that is appropriate.

MICHAEL BOTTING
Editor

66 Solomon

TEXT

1 Kings 3:3–15.

AIM

To study an example of life and prayer in a man with new responsibilities.

PREPARATION

Make two large circles out of card. The underneath one should be thicker and firmer than the top one and able to rotate while the top one with the added piece below stays fixed (see diagram). Cut-out day-glo lettering is used throughout. The words *prayer* and *life* have a detachable flap over them so that they are obscured at the beginning of the talk. Monopoly money is stapled on in the third quadrant and also the 'un' of unselfish is covered. The background of the second quadrant can be a scroll. (Note: Once a firm back circle has been made it can be reversed and used for another visual aid in a similar style.)

PRESENTATION

Remind people of where the story comes in the Bible. (Uncover the word *Life* and remove detachable quadrant with text on it.)

We learn two wonderful things about the life of Solomon:

(a) He *loved God* (v.3a).

(b) He *kept God's Law* (v.3b. rotate back circle to reveal second

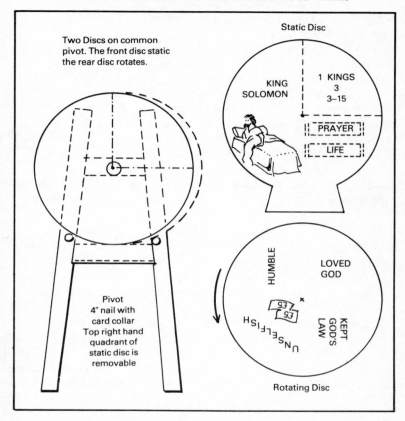

Two Discs on common pivot. The front disc static the rear disc rotates.

Static Disc

KING SOLOMON

1 KINGS 3 3–15

PRAYER

LIFE

Pivot
4" nail with card collar
Top right hand quadrant of static disc is removable

HUMBLE

LOVED GOD

UNSELFISH

KEPT GOD'S LAW

Rotating Disc

quadrant). He had learnt so many good things from his father—King David. Above all he had learnt about the Law of God. Explain that he would only have had a few books—not the whole Bible that we have and that the books were written on scrolls.

Although he tried to love God and follow what God wanted he had his faults. His worship was not pure and not exactly what God wanted (v.3c).

Now we move on to a particular experience in Solomon's prayer life. Describe the journey to Gibeon. He would be going to bed tired and with worries on his mind about his new responsibilities as king after the death of his father. (Uncover the word *Prayer* so that the front now reads *Prayer Life*.)

You may not normally think of praying while you are sleeping— Solomon evidently did! God asks him a question (v.5).

In his answering prayer there are two great lessons about prayer:

(c) (Rotate to third quadrant.) His prayer could have been selfish. He could have asked for money and other things like fame. (Monopoly money is to illustrate that.)

(Uncover 'un' so that the word reads *Unselfish*.) Look at v.9 which tells us what he actually asked for. Look at God's answer in vv.11–13.

He was *unselfish* in his praying.

(d) (Turn to last quadrant.) He was *humble*. Look at v.7. We see this in the way that he prayed. He was not big-headed or demanding.

Conclusion

Go through four points again, but refer to ourselves. Ask whether it could be said of us that we *love God* and *keep his Law* (the Bible).

· And when we have new responsibilities, (here adult and children's examples could be used) do we pray *unselfishly* and *humbly*.

God's answer to Solomon was more than he asked. It pleases God when we ask not for selfish things but for good things and when we seek to love and obey him.

JOHN TOWNSEND
Kensal Rise, London

67 Joash

TEXT

2 Chron 23:3–11, 16, 20–21; 24:1, 2; Mt 18:1–7, 10–14.

AIM

To stress the importance of the right treatment of children to prepare them for the future.

PREPARATION

Draw pictures either on large pieces of paper with some on small pieces (or on acetate sheets for an overhead projector).

(1) Scene with temple steps, pillar and two guards
(2) Jehoiada the priest, and Joash the boy king with, separately,
(3) crown in Jehoiada's hand
(4) trumpeter
(5) two soldiers with drawn swords (larger than other figures as they will be closer to the viewer)
(6) small scroll to go later into Joash's hand
(7) large scroll to show congregation
(8) Temple interior scene with altar and candlestick
(9) couple to represent the people

Headings can also be prepared for display (italics below).

You will also find it helpful to read 2 Chron 21 and 22 to give the background to the story. Like many other passages in the Old Testament these chapters show how God preserved the ancestral line from David to Jesus. In this instance it was the godly priest Jehoiada and his wife Jehosheba (GNB spelling) whom God used to save Joash, Ahaziah's youngest son, from death at the hands of the jealous Queen Athaliah, and so preserved him to be king.

PRESENTATION

Jesus emphasised the importance of children. Jehoiada, priest of Israel, made the child Joash important and prepared him for godly responsibilities.

(a) *Recognition*

Jehoiada recognised the young heir to the throne personally and treated him with great respect. He called the leaders of the clans, or tribes, of Judah and the Levites and planned for his public recognition. The place for acclaiming the new king was a special column at the Temple entrance (1) and Jehoiada brought Joash out (2) and placed the crown (3) on his head. Then the trumpeters (4) blew a fanfare.

Jesus wants children in his family. Do you recognise their importance?

(b) *Protection*

Jehoiada made sure that King Joash would be properly protected from his enemies, especially Queen Athaliah. The Levites were commanded to stand guard round the King with drawn swords (5) wherever he went.

Jesus said angels were watching over God's children (Mt 18:10). Do you claim protection for your children?

(c) *Instruction*

Jehoiada gave Joash instruction in the laws governing kingship (6). Jewish children were instructed from Bible scrolls like this (7). We have the Bible to give to our children. From it we need to give instruction in living happy, useful, holy lives. This must include regular worship in the holy place (8).

(d) *Dedication*

Jehoiada, the priest, got King Joash (2) and the people (9) to join him in the temple to make a covenant with God to be God's people. We

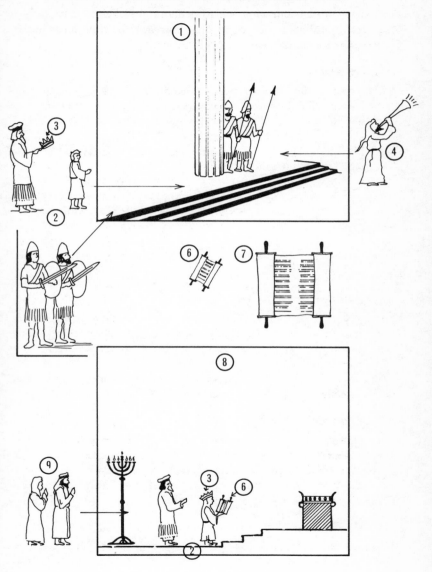

must encourage our children to dedicate themselves personally to God and publicly to his people, the Church. Each church has its own ceremony for this public act of commitment.

(e) *Optional conclusion*

As a result of these things there followed:-
- ° Peace (23:21) Peace in the land because of peace with God
- ° Pleasure (24:10) Pleasure in giving. Pleasure for God (24:2)
- ° Plenty (24:11) Plenty for God's work
- ° Peril (24:17) Perils of spiritual decline when separated from the word of God through the priest.

PETER BARTON
Malmesbury

68 Barnabas

TEXT
Acts 4:32–37, Acts 11:19–26, Acts 9:26–28.

AIM

To learn lessons about being helpful to one another in the life of the local church.

PREPARATION

This is designed for use on a teazlegraph board. Picture of Barnabas is enlarged from *Help, I can't Draw* (Vol.I, No.87, see appendix.) Three other pictures of Barnabas and map of Cyprus are prepared. Also lettering for the two words.

PRESENTATION

Introduce Barnabas and where he came from. (Put him on board.)

(a) He was a *GOOD* man. (Put up word.) Explain that so often we think of goodness as dull, dreary and quite unattractive. (Read Acts 11:24.) Barnabas allowed the Holy Spirit to change him into a great character. His goodness was attractive. There are two ways in which this can be seen.

° *His friendliness* (Acts 11:22). (Put up picture of him talking to teenagers.) They sent Barnabas, not just because he could teach, but also because he got on so well with people.

° His generosity (Acts 4:36, 37). (Put up map of Cyprus.) Talk about how we can be generous within the church family.

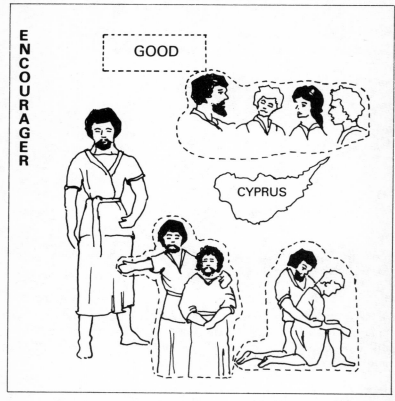

(b) He was an *ENCOURAGER* (Acts 4:36). (Put up word.)
His real name was Joseph. Barnabas—encourager was a nickname—
I wonder whether our nicknames show anything good about us.
   ° *He helped to introduce Paul into the church family* when others were
     suspicious of him (Acts 9:26–28). (Put up pictures of Barnabas
     with his arm around Paul.) We can do a lot to help new Christians
     feel welcome in the Church family.
   ° *He lifted the mood of people.* (Put up picture of him lifting up
     someone.) Acts 11:23—a teacher who urged them on. V.26—he
     obtained more help so that the church could grow—he was
     humble enough to look round for a more gifted teacher.

Conclusion

Two great qualities—attractive goodness and an encourager...
qualities that we can put into action in our local church.

Note: (This style of presentation can be adapted for use with other
characters.)

JOHN TOWNSEND
Kensal Rise, London

69 John Mark

Text
Acts 12:12, 13:13, 2 Tim 4:11 and 1 Pet 5:13.

Aim

To discover what we can learn from the life of John Mark as revealed in the Bible.

Preparation

If possible obtain props and clothing used by Sherlock Holmes e.g. deer-stalker hat, cloak with cape (I borrowed one from the local theatre for a small fee), a magnifying glass and pipe. The last I made out of cardboard as the authentic design seemed non-existent.

Also prepare four cards bent in half. On the inside have the four texts above written boldly, one on each. On the outside of the card have *CLUE A, B* etc. These should be given secretly to four children before the Family Service begins.

Prepare material for the teazlegraph board—*JOHN MARK, KOLOBO-DACTYLUS*. Other words: *Christian homes, Useful disciple, Writer*. Pictures of cross, praying hands, a modern house, a ship with single sail, four symbolic people i.e. in different colours and arrows and two people poring over scrolls. The word Gospel i.e. on an open book and a hand where the little finger can be pulled away.

PRESENTATION

How many of you like reading detective stories? A famous archbishop said he enjoyed them providing the body turned up in the first chapter.

We are going to do some detective work this morning so we had better be dressed for the part. (Put on detective outfit.)

We are going to discover all we can about *KOLOBO-DACTYLUS!* Who knows who that might be? (Put word in middle of teazlegraph board.) Well I will tell you why he was called that later. His other name was *JOHN MARK*. (Put at top of teazlegraph board.)

Now what can we discover about him? Perhaps from his Gospel? No, that's no use because there's nothing about the author there. It begins 'The beginning of the Gospel of Jesus Christ the Son of God'. The writer was more interested in Jesus than himself, though I believe Mark does leave his mark! Ask for:-

Clue A: (Acts 12:12)

Get congregation to look it up in their Bibles. Ask what we can learn about Mark's home? Draw out that it was large, hospitable and a praying one. Put on teazlegraph board *Christian home* with house and cross and praying hands over it.

I believe this may have been the home where the Lord's Supper was first celebrated. In the excitement typical of Passover time, when Jesus and the disciples sang a hymn and went to the Mount of Olives, Mark followed them and was the young boy mentioned in Mk 14:51–52. If not, who was it and why was it written?

So John Mark came from a happy Christian home. What a privilege. Do we? If so, do we thank God for it?

Clue B: (Acts 13:13)

Tell the sad story of the first missionary journey and John Mark returning home before it was finished. (Put up under *KOLOBO-DACTYLUS* the ship with two men going in one direction—i.e. Paul and Barnabas—and another—John Mark—going in the other: arrows indicating direction.) Look up Acts 15:36–39 and show how Mark's desertion caused a split and quarrel between Paul and Barnabas. In

215

the Roman Army he could have had his little finger chopped off. So he was nicknamed Kolobo-Dactylus meaning maimed in the finger. (Put up hand and remove finger.)

Clue C: (2 Tim 4:11 and put up on teazlegraph board *Useful disciple*)

Mark may have deserted, but he came back and was obviously forgiven and became very useful to Paul in the latter days of his ministry in prison. (Put up the remaining figure, preferably in bright yellow.)

Clue D: (1 Pet 5:13)

'My son Mark'. Why *son?* Perhaps Peter led him to Jesus in his home. he also helped Peter write a gospel which has lots about Peter in it, including his faults.

Well, what would be our verdict on John Mark? Would we be proud to have his record? He may have had failings but he came back to the Lord and helped Barnabas on the mission field, Paul in prison and Peter write a gospel. Put up Gospel-*writer* and two men with scrolls.

> *We are writing a gospel, a chapter each day*
> *In all that we do, in all that we say.*
> *Men read what we write, whether faithless or true*
> *Pray, what's the gospel according to you?*

MICHAEL BOTTING
Editor

70 Stephen

To tell the story of Stephen, the first Christian martyr, as recorded in Acts 6–7.

PREPARATION

In place of the Lesson, show the film-strip produced by Concordia, (Cat. No.CCF.430) using sound recorded by your own congregation. Have the following words on teazle-covered cards for use on the teazlegraph board *Stephen, He served, He spoke, He suffered.* Cut out from gold paper or card a small crown, and put velcro on the back.

PRESENTATION

If you are giving this talk on the day after Christmas then you could ask the congregation if they know what day it is, and perhaps make reference to the carol *Good King Wenceslas.* Otherwise simply refer to the film-strip they have seen. Put up, not quite at the top of the board, the name *Stephen*. There are just three brief things I want to mention about this great man. (Put up the words as you come to them.)

He served

Explain about the widows getting neglected and there being no state social security provision. Stephen was appointed one of the seven deacons to deal with the problem. Some people think that the only use they can be in the church is to hand out hymn-books or count the collection. Someone has to do that job, but there are a whole range of jobs in which Christians can serve in the church as well.

He spoke

Refer to 6:10 and the defence Stephen made in chapter 7. All of us may be called upon to defend our faith at sometime or other. Stephen was appalled at the way the Temple was worshipped at the expense of God himself. He aimed to show that 'God did not dwell in houses made with hands'. The points he made were that Abraham, Isaac and Israel were nomads; Moses built the tabernacle, but there was no place for God in it; David was prevented from building the Temple, and though Solomon his son did, it was second best and Solomon himself acknowledged God had no specific place in it.

Today we can be in danger of idolising church and cathedral buildings as if God had a reserved seat in them. Perhaps tell the story of the boy who was taken to church by his mother for the first time. Mystified by the extraordinary building he tried to ask questions, but was told to be quiet. On asking why he should keep quiet he was told he was in God's house. 'Well if I was God I'd move!' was his reply. God is surely in our church building, but then he is everywhere, and especially where two or three are gathered in his name.

He suffered

Mention that there are various similarities between Stephen's death and that of the Master whom he served: the blasphemy charge, the illegality of the whole event, the forgiving of the murderers, the committing of the life into the hands of God/Jesus. We might be tempted to say 'What a waste!' No, for as a result the gospel spread and the greatest Christian missionary the church has ever had was obviously considerably influenced—Saul of Tarsus, who became Paul the apostle.

Jesus said to the Church at Smyrna 'Be faithful unto death, and I will give you the crown of life' (Rev 2:10). Stephen lived up to his name, for it means crown. Place the visual of the crown over Stephen's name at the top of your board.

MICHAEL BOTTING
Editor

71 Timothy Man of God

TEXT
2 Tim 1:1–7, 2:1–7, 3:14–17.
This talk could be used on Mothering Sunday.

AIM

To discover all we can about the Christian life as revealed in the life of Timothy.

PREPARATION

Prepare for use on a teazlegraph board the following words (with suggested colours in day-glo card):

TIMOTHY, shy, sick (green)
MAN of GOD, brave, loyal (red)
home (pink), *Scriptures* (white)
friendship (buff), *Spirit* (red and orange alternately)
effort (yellow)

Prepare also the following drawings after the style of the line figures in TEV by Annie Vallotton: a sickly boy (green), a cross and soldier (red), a mother in attitude of prayer (pink), a scroll, two people greeting each other (buff), flames (in red and orange), an athlete (yellow). Also take a cover of say a Good News Bible and stick velcro on the back.

The way all these visual aids are arranged on the teazlegraph board will depend on its size. In any case the whole plan should be worked out carefully before hand and everything taken off and filed in the order that the items will be required. I would suggest that the green and red items are shown on one side of your board and the remainder on the reverse side. In the presentation which follows, the visual aids are in italics when they should be placed on the board.

PRESENTATION

We who are parents, what do we really want for our children? To be happy? Of course, but how? A secure job, adequate money and successful marriage—these may all help towards a happy life.

I want to suggest a worthier aim—that they become men and women of God. This may possibly sound dull, but if Jesus promised us the abundant life (Jn 10:10) then surely it should be the best and happiest life.

Let's see how this worked out in the life of a biblical character like

TIMOTHY (Place top left of board)

Humanly speaking he was a timid, *shy* boy, not naturally very courageous, rather easily tempted, perhaps easily led. He was prone to illness, especially tummy-ache (put up *sick*). He was brought up in Lystra in Asia Minor, his mother being a Jewess who taught him the Old Testament, probably helped by his grandmother. His father was a Greek. Timothy became a

MAN of GOD (Place to right of board)

How did the change come about? Talk about the apostle Paul's visit on his first missionary journey as a result of which Timothy, his mother and grandmother all became Christians. (Put up *cross* on right of the boy and words *shy* and *sick*.)

Later, on his second missionary journey, Paul called at Lystra and received a very good report on Timothy, so took him with him. Timothy became a minister and *soldier* of Jesus Christ.

Refer to his bravery in service with Paul and Silas (put up *brave*). Later Paul wrote to the Philippians: 'He is the only one who shares any feelings and who really cares about you.... He has proved his worth.' (Phil 2:20 & 22 TEV.) (Put up *loyal*.)

At the end of Paul's life, when he was in prison and expecting death he wrote: 'Do your best to come to me soon.' So Timothy, shy and sick, became the brave, loyal successor of the greatest Christian missionary of all time.

WHAT WAS THE SECRET? (Reverse teazlegraph board)

In one sense the single answer was that Timothy became a Christian. But that needs unpacking. Suggest and briefly comment on the following factors and apply to congregation.

(a) *Home* (put up *praying woman*). Refer to mother's prayers and example.

(b) *Scriptures* (put up *scroll* and TEV cover). Quote from 2 Tim 3:15–17. Timothy probably wrote down at least three of Paul's letters and two were sent to him. He would have heard much of the Old Testament from his mother.

(c) *Friendship* (put up *two people greeting*). Paul and Timothy were deeply attached to each other (2 Tim 1:4). The importance of the right friends.

(d) *Spirit* (put up *flames*). Refer to the gift of God (2 Tim 1:6–7). The Holy Spirit is several times referred to as a fire that must not be quenched but rekindled.

(e) *Effort* (put up athlete). Refer to 2 Tim 2:5 and Phil 2:12b–13. All the things we have been thinking about—the influence of home, scriptures, friends and the Holy Spirit will be useless unless we co-operate and this will mean effort. So may we all enjoy the abundant life of men and women of God.

MICHAEL BOTTING
Editor

72 The tower of Babel

TEXT
Gen 11:1–9.

AIM

That the congregation will grasp the difference between man's achievements and the grace of God.

PREPARATION

The outline that follows is partly based on information to be found in the article 'Babel' in the *New Bible Dictionary* (IVP). Ideally use a two-sided visual aid board, or have the two models on either side of a large board.

Left hand side
Assembled but covered before the talk starts.

Right hand side
Make the tower in separate pieces of stiff paper each edged with black marker or paint and divided into 'bricks' about two inches square. The words will be filled in using ladder lettering, with quarter inch paint brush and black powder paint.

PRESENTATION

Introduction

Who makes the rules and plans in your house? Christians belong to

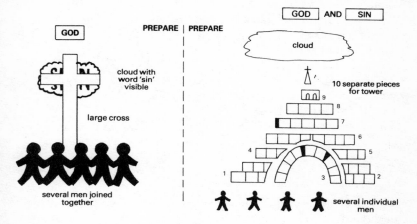

another family, the family of God, where God should make the plans for us; God wants us to work with him.

(a) *The story of Babel*

God created people to be his family, he made a special agreement with Noah—the covenant—to remind Noah and his people that they were part of God's family, but the people soon forgot this and disobeyed God and made their own plans. They settled in a place called Shinar and were ruled by Nimrod who was a great city builder.

(b) *The building*

The people began building; they had brick factories and were all very busy. It is easy to forget God if we are too busy. (Start building your tower as you tell the story–pieces 1 and 2. What was the city called?

Do you know what Babel means? (Piece 3)

It means 'Gate of God' (fill in words around the gate). The people called it

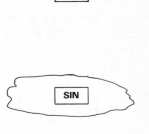

that, to salve their consciences. They thought God would be pleased. They continued building (pieces 4 and 5). They built a beautiful city although God had not told them to (piece 6). They built up the tower (pieces 7 and 8). Why? To show how clever they were and to make a name for themselves. They put a temple on the top (piece 9).

They did not neglect religion, but the temple was at the top, so that God would not interfere with their life in the city. They kept God at a distance.

(c) *The people's reaction*

They probably said something like 'Aren't we clever!' and 'We don't need God'. The pop song of the day could well have been 'Glory to man in the highest'. No doubt life in the city was not all happiness. There would have been arguments, jealousy, drunkenness, nervous breakdowns...and death. The city was civilised, but godless.

Nimrod was very pleased. He could have sung, 'Mine is the kingdom, the power and the glory.' His tower was so high it nearly reached the clouds (add the cloud).

But the people had cut themselves off from God (add God) by their sin (add sin across the cloud).

(d) *God's reaction*

God saw not a beautiful city, but ruined godless lives and a place that was becoming worse because he was left out of their plans.

(e) *God's judgement*

Before they got any worse God stepped in and confused their language. They had not listened to God, so now they could not understand one another. The building stopped, the city fell into ruins and the people separated and became lonely people (add separate figures).

(f) *Modern Babel*

People still build Babels today, by ignoring God's plans and trying to build a better world on their own. (Fill in the following words, or others appropriate to your situation)

 - some people are too busy, or their work is too demanding to have time for God.

 - some people's homes are all important. They spend all their time on DIY. They may have beautiful, but godless homes.

- to some people their studies are all that matter. You can become very clever, but not know God.

- some spend all their time being good and kind, but in itself, not even goodness will build the way to God.

Many people add a little religion (add spire with cross–piece 10) to their lives and think God will be pleased. None of these things are sufficient to build a tower to God because we all sin and God is perfect.

In our modern world there are plenty of Babels: bigger and better buildings, aeroplanes, bombs, standard of living. Yet so many people are confused, they cannot communicate, cannot understand themselves or others and so experience breakdowns. This is God's judgement on a world that has turned its back on him.

(g) *God's way*

(Uncover left hand side of board) God has reached down to us. He became a man, and through the cross, sin is forgiven and man linked with God. In Christ we find a unity, even if we speak different languages.

Conclusion

Are you trying to build your own Babel? Living your own life by your own effort and plans with just an occasional thought for God? Or is Jesus in the centre of your life, forgiving you, planning your life and making you a member of God's family?

JUDITH ROSE
Bradford

73 Getting it straight—the plumbline

TEXT

Amos 7:7–9.

AIM

To teach that we need a perfect standard by which to measure our lives.

PREPARATION

Obtain or make a simple plumbline. Have a piece of elastic to hand. Cover some red day-glo card with some similar coloured red paper. Cut one fairly large piece off and, using yellow day-glo paper, stick onto it the word *JESUS*. Cut up the remainder of the card to look like bricks of a wall with white paint for the concrete or cement between the bricks as illustrated (1). On these 'bricks' write the words:*theft, greed, hate, impurity, idolatry*. On the reverse sides have the words: *peace, joy, love, patience, goodness*. Stick velcro on the white parts of the 'bricks' on both sides. See wall when built this way round (2). Erect the teazlegraph board.

PRESENTATION

Who knows what a plumbline is? Explain about the name from the Latin *plumbum* meaning lead. If we were wanting to make sure a wall was built straight ask if this bit of elastic would be any use? Confirm that we need something like a plumbline that is always straight.

Introduce Amos and explain that he had a vision of a man building a wall with a plumbline. He saw how the people of Israel, many years before Jesus came, were building their lives as individuals and as a nation. They were not straight. Refer to the sins of the nation and as you speak of them bring each up to date. Put the 'bricks' with the various sins on them on your board to make a wall that is obviously not straight. Use the plumbline to make it even more obvious the wall is not straight.

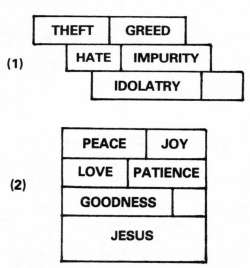

Ask what is God's plumbline and draw out the twofold answer (a) God's law: Deut 4:7–8 (b) Jesus: Jn 8:46, Acts 17:30–31. These are the perfect standards and like the plumbline will never change. By these will God judge us.

Refer to other possible standards that in fact are unreliable: (a) *Conscience*. The trouble is that, like a computer, it will only turn out what has been fed into it. It has been known for the children of thieves to have their consciences prick them because they had *not* been out stealing. (b) *Company*. The trouble is that, like the chameleon, standards can so easily change colour according to who joins. (c) *The World*. The standard here is usually what everybody else is doing. It is fatal when we fix on our own standards and not God's.

When we compare ourselves with God's standard we should make three discoveries:

° *We are not straight, but guilty of sin.* Sin will keep us out of heaven, because it is a perfect place.

° *We need to come to Jesus for forgiveness.* He is the only person who has done anything to answer the problem of sin. Put up the foundation for a new building on the board with the word *JESUS* on it.

° *We need to live according to God's perfect standard.* Just as some people make the mistake of trying to get to heaven without Jesus, some think that once they have accepted him as Saviour, they can live as they like (see Mt 7:21).

Explain that the only evidence that Jesus is our Saviour is if the fruit of the Spirit appears. Turn the words round and then rebuild on the foundation of Jesus a wall with straight sides. Apply the plumbline. As Christians we have to show our thankfulness for our salvation by living obedient lives.

MICHAEL BOTTING
Editor

74 The wedding at Cana

TEXT

Jn 2:1–11.

AIM

To teach the story of the wedding and the meaning of the words
'Whatever he says to you, do it', which are the words Mary spoke to
the servants about Jesus.

PREPARATION

You need to have a large piece of cardboard, and the shape of four
bottles cut out of it so:

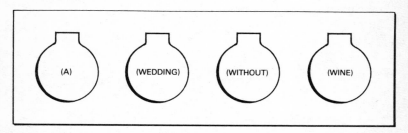

(a) Take a second piece of cardboard of the same size and staple or
fix it with tape behind the first piece to make a pocket. You now have a
space between the two.

(b) Into this pocket put sheets of black, white, light blue, red and
white cartridge paper in that order, front to back, so that when you

look at the visual aid from the front you see the black shapes of four bottles in the holes.

(c) As the talk proceeds lift out of the top the black paper so as to slowly reveal the words *a wedding without wine*.

(d) Lift up the white to show the light blue underneath. From a distance it actually looks as though the bottles are filling with water as you lift out the black.

(e) Lift out the blue to reveal the red and again it looks as though the bottles are slowly changing to wine.

(f) Finally take out the red to reveal the white. On this write words to appear through the holes as follows:

(g) Have ready an empty fountain pen or biro and a wedding ring.

(h) If the organist will oblige ask him to play a Wedding March.

PRESENTATION

(a) Begin by saying you have an invitation for the congregation to come to something special. Ask them to guess what it is by listening to the music. (Here the organist should play the tune of a Wedding March.) If this creates no response produce a wedding ring. Explain how joyful weddings are and say that all the best ones have a wedding breakfast or meal which has food and (usually) wine.

The wedding you want to invite them to was unusual—show them the black outlines of the bottles—take out the black paper and reveal the words in the holes: *A WEDDING WITHOUT WINE*.

Some weddings are even worse because they are weddings without Jesus—he being the most important person to have in your life. Some people are like the waterpots, empty. (Produce your empty pen to show how useless it is.) You can draw a similar example from the petrol in the tank of a car. This is how a marriage is without Jesus.

(b) Say you will tell them the secret of this wedding and all good marriages. Silently mouth the words: *Whatever he says to you, do it*. Ask the congregation if they understood. If someone says 'yes', tell him to keep it to himself until later. If they shake their heads, say you will show them more clearly later.

Jesus told the servants to fill the waterpots with water. (Pull out the white paper slowly to reveal the blue.)

The water changed into wine. (Pull out the blue to reveal the red.)

The guests said the best was kept until last and you have kept the secret of the wedding until last. (Pull out the red to reveal the words: *'Whatever he says to you, do it'*.) Explain that to do the Lord's will is the secret of a good life.

CHRIS PORTEOUS
Beckenham

75 Hands

Mk 10:13–16   - children in his arms
Mk 1:40–43   - healing a leper
Jn 13:3–5   - washing disciples' feet.

AIM

To demonstrate that Jesus used his hands in the course of his ministry, and that we should use ours.

PREPARATION

Scarf for blindfold
Stamp pad, ink and paper
Sheets of paper about six inches square
Writing in Braille
Flannel and towel

PRESENTATION

(a) *The use of our hands*

Ask a child to go and collect some item in the church but have him/her blindfolded. Ask everyone to notice how the child stretches out hands to feel the way.

Invite another child to give finger prints, using the stamp pad, and explain how intricate our hands are. They can be used by the police in identificaton.

233

Each child can then be asked to look at his own hand and be given the square of paper to draw round it.

Finally, a piece of Braille can be produced (I invited a blind person to do this for me, and he also stretched out his hand to move towards me.) Show how important it is for a blind person to understand what he cannot see.

(b) *Jesus' hands*

Take the three readings from above. Invite children and adults to enact each story in turn, and give a commentary on the story to show how Jesus used his hands.

(c) *Our hands for Jesus*

The children can now be invited to list the many ways in which their hands can be used to do God's work. (If this forms the basis of a whole service, rather than merely a talk, then varied aspects of life, at home and on the mission field could be demonstrated at this point.)

BOB METCALF
Liverpool

76 A story for our time—(Given during the Golden Jubilee of St George's Crypt)

TEXT

Lk 10:25–37.

AIM

To teach that the gospel of God's love for us in Christ must have outward response in our love for our neighbour.

PREPARATION

Though this talk was prepared for a specific and unique occasion it could be adapted easily for any occasion when the social implications of the gospel need to be taught. The visuals for the talk were all painted by an artist in the congregation for use on the teazlegraph board. The background at the top right-hand corner of the picture which includes *HEAVEN* is that of Leeds, where the Crypt is situated. Velcro was stuck on the backs of all the visuals.

PRESENTATION

A clever lawyer (at least he thought he was clever) was trying to catch Jesus out with a religious question. 'How do you get to heaven?' he asked. Of course he thought he knew all the possible answers Jesus could give. Jesus simply asked him what was written in the Bible (our Old Testament). The lawyer was really embarrassed by that, for Jesus was treating him like a child.

He blurts out the two great commandments on loving God and neighbour. 'That's right' says Jesus, 'Do that and you'll get to heaven.'

Sounds easy enough, but the lawyer cannot let Jesus have the last word, so he asks who his neighbour is. Jesus replies with one of his best known stories, the Good Samaritan. Tell the story in your own words, putting up the visuals at the appropriate moments.

Modern application

We are all on a journey. (Reverse the board and put up heaven and the other visuals as you refer to them.) Like the lawyer we want to know how to get to heaven. But like the route to Jericho the journey is hazardous. Special perils in the city are unemployment, gambling and drink, which can leave us half dead.

Along comes the *gospel preacher* on his way to a great conference to tell people about the love of God and how Jesus came to save sinners. Such people know they must get their priorities right. Too many people have just a social gospel. He passes by on the other side.

Then along comes an *average church member*. He thinks to himself that he does plenty for the church, and there are others to look after tramps. He, too, passes by on the other side.

Finally along comes the modern *Good Samaritan*. His background is a bit uncertain, and one cannot be quite sure his beliefs are entirely orthodox. However he goes over to the man on the ground, loves and cares for him and gets him all the help he needs.

The talk could be concluded with the story of Bill, as told by Rebecca Manley Pippert in *Out of the Saltshaker* (IVP) pp.177–8.

MICHAEL BOTTING
Editor

77 No longer strangers

TEXT

Eph 2:11–22.

AIM

The Gospel of Christ brings peace with God and our fellow human beings, whoever they are.

PREPARATION

This talk was specially written with the work of St George's Crypt in mind, but it could be adapted to any appropriate situation. An artist in the congregation painted all the visuals as illustrated. They were all backed with velcro for use on the teazlegraph board.

PRESENTATION

(a) *Walls* (Have the complete wall already on the board at the start of the talk.)

Ask who is brave enough to put up their hand to admit they have been sent out of the room for bad behaviour, whether at home or school. (Put up one's own hand if it is true.) Refer to the problems of loneliness such treatment brings and the loneliness of high-rise flats, solitary confinement in prison etc.

Mention the wall on the board and ask if anyone can think of walls of separation. The Berlin wall will almost certainly be mentioned. Then refer to the 'dividing wall of hostility' in Jerusalem (Eph 2:14).

State that two notices have recently been discovered with their stark message, not 'Trespassers will be prosecuted', but 'Trespassers will be EXECUTED'! Explain that there was a division between Jews and Gentiles in Jesus' day, as there still is to some extent today. (Put up the Jew and the Gentile on either side of the wall.) An even more important wall was inside the Temple in Jerusalem: the great veil that hung between the Holy Place and the Holy of Holies. Explain the layout of the Tabernacle and Temple.

The world is separated from God because of sin. (Put up God and the world on the board.) However there can be walls between us that are not made of bricks, walls created by our hates, jealousies, refusing to hear each others' point of view or to forgive, walls between classes and cultures, respectable and otherwise. (Put up respectable and non-respectable men.)

(b) *The breaking down of the wall*

Jesus came to bring peace. Refer to various texts that make that point, such as Is 9:6, Lk 2:14, Jn 20:21, Rom 5:1. Then refer back to the Temple veil and Day of Atonement and lead on to the cross, which

means that we now have access to God. (Remove the cross from the wall.) The world can have real peace with God, not by attempting to obey God perfectly, which we could never do, but by accepting what Jesus has done for us on the cross. Man is no longer a stranger to brother man.

(c) *Temple* (Remove the people from the board and reverse the board.)

Explain that Paul used various illustrations to show how we all become one: we are all citizens of the same kingdom and members of the same body. He tells the Ephesians that we are also all bricks in the same building—a temple to the Lord. Ask what a solid firm building needs? Obtain the answer 'Foundation' and point out from 2:20 that this means the teaching of the apostles and prophets.

Refer to the teaching given in your church from the Bible and put up the visual. Proceed to build up the Church/Temple as illustrated, referring to Christ as the cornerstone (2:20). Build in the four people previously shown divided by the wall. Finally refer to the cement of the Holy Spirit (2:21–22) and place the dove on the board. Various relationships are mentioned in Ephesians: husbands and wives, parents and children, employers and employees. (See 5:21–6:9.)

MICHAEL BOTTING
Editor

78 Biblical fools

TEXT
Ps 14:1, Lk 12:20, 1 Cor 4:10.

PREPARATION

The illustrations were painted specially for this talk, the man on the left being the Psalmist, the man in the centre the Rich Fool of Jesus' parable in Lk 12, and the man on the right the 'Fool for Christ's sake'. Each visual had velcro on the back for use on the teazlegraph board. This talk is suitable for use near April Fool's Day.

PRESENTATION

I want to introduce you to three fools referred to in the Bible and to ask which one most fits you.

(a) *The fool who said there was no God*

Refer to Ps 14 and put up the Psalmist on the board. The Psalmist was really saying that some said 'God does not matter', but what they really meant was 'Sin does not matter'. Explain that sin obviously does matter very much because of two things. *Conscience:* why were we given this moral regulator if sin is unimportant? *The cross of Christ:* why did Jesus die on the cross if sin doesn't matter? Do you say sin doesn't matter because God does not matter? If so, the Bible calls you a fool.

(b) *The rich fool*

Ask who can tell me about another fool in the Bible. (I could ask this question with reasonable certainty of getting an answer, because the story in Lk 12 had been read as the Lesson. Tell the story again in your own words, putting up the visuals as they become relevant.) Most people would call the man a very able administrator and anything but a fool. But God saw his life was just concerned with himself, his money, his pleasure, whereas Jesus came to bring abundant life, eternal life, a new quality of life that never ends, so he was foolishly missing the best.

The other reason why he was a fool was because he forgot that he did not know how long was his life. Refer to someone known to the congregation who has recently died unexpectedly and young. When the rich man died his wealth was no use to him. Someone once asked, on hearing that a millionnaire had died, how much he had left, to which the answer was given 'Everything'.

Are you just living for yourself and this life, with no thought for God and eternity? Then God calls you a fool.

(c) *The wise fool*

Quote 1 Cor 4:10 (Put up the clown.) Refer to the musical *Godspell* which shocked some people, because the clown represented Jesus. In

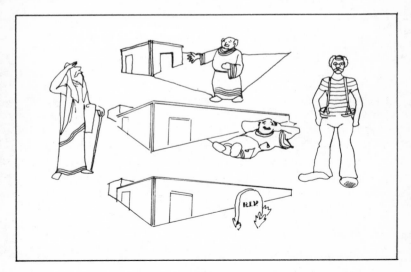

one sense what a foolish life he lived. He lived totally for other people, never giving any thought for himself; he made no attempt to seek high office, never got married, settled down or reared a family. Knowing perfectly well the religious leaders were plotting his murder he walked straight into their trap and refused to defend himself when on trial. The religious leaders called him mad, yet he challenged the world to follow him, and millions down the centuries have done so and found abundant life as a consequence—like the apostle Paul, who admitted he was a fool for Christ's sake.

How does such a foolish life begin? Refer to 1 Corinthians 1:18 and explain briefly about the cross. Those who follow Jesus will be seen as foolish in the world's eyes. At baptism we are told not to be ashamed to be Christ's soldiers and servants. End with the story of the hot-gospeller who wore sandwich boards. On one side was 'A fool for Christ's sake'. But when people turned round to see what was on his back they read 'Whose fool are you?'

MICHAEL BOTTING
Editor

Appendix: Books, aids and equipment

BOOKS

Michael Botting with John Tigwell, *Reaching the Families*, (Falcon) Revised edition 1976, which itself contains an Appendix with many details of books, aids and equipment.

James Kennedy, *Evangelism Explosion*. Full details from E. E. (G.B.), 228 Shirley Road, Southampton, SO1 3HR.

Kenneth Stevenson, *Family Services*, Alcuin Club Manual No.3.

John Stott, *I Believe in Preaching* (Hodder & Stoughton).

Clifford Warne, *Know How to Tell a Story* (Scripture Union).

Michael Wooderson, *Good News down the Street* (Grove Booklets, Pastoral Series 9).

Further information can be found in CIO publications *All Generations* from The Offchurch Group and *Live, Learn and Worship* from The Wadderton Group. Scripture Union also publish teaching material especially designed for Family Services. Write to SU House, 130 City Road, London EC1V 2NJ.

DRAMA

Paul Burbridge and Murrey Watts, *Time to Act* and *Lightning Sketches* (Hodder & Stoughton).

Gillian Grinham, *Know How to use Drama in Church* (Scripture Union).

Andy Kelso, *Drama in Worship* (Grove Booklet on Ministry and Worship 35).

Alan MacDonald and Steve Stickley, *The Drama Recipe Book* (Minstrel, Kingsway).

Nick McIvor, *The Greatest Burger Ever Sold* (Minstrel, Kingsway).

Nick Page, *The Dame Cecily Spume Drama Notebook* and *Dame Cecily The First Farewell Tour*, (Minstrel, Kingsway).

Dave Seymour, *One Flew Over the Church Spire*, (Minstrel, Kingsway).

EQUIPMENT

Information on projectors is available from The Education Foundation for Visual Aids (Centre and Library) at Paxton Place, Gipsy Road, London SE27 9SR.

For information on Teazlegraph, see the Introduction.

Marler Haley ExpoSystems Ltd., 7 High Street, Barnet, Herts EN5 5UF produce boards and other materials similar to teazlegraph.

Magiboards Ltd., 42 Wates Way, Willow Lane Industrial Estate, Mitcham, Surrey CR4 4TA provide a wide range of visual aid boards and accompanying materials.

Primaboard, Ashford Road, Ashford, Middx., produce vitrous Enamel Steel Marker Board and accompanying materials.

Velcro for teazlegraph boards can be bought more economically in long rolls from the manufacturers: Sleectus Ltd., Biddulph, Stoke-on-Trent, ST8 7SH.

FILM-STRIPS

Cine Screens Ltd., Leighton Road, Linsdale, Leighton Buzzard, Beds LU7 7LF, (0525 372775) provide ideal translucent material for daylight screens as well as other screen materials. Write for their catalogue.

Clearvue Projection Co., 92 Stroud Green Road, London N4 3EN, supply an excellent Trojan stand for projectors.

Film-strips can be obtained from quite a number of sources such as:

Church Army, Audio Visual Aids units, Independence Road, Blackheath, London SE3 9LG.

Carwel Audio Visual Aids Ltd., PO Box 55, Wallington, Surrey (01 647 5161).

Concordia Publishing House, The Garden House, Hothorp Hall, Theddingworth, Lutterworth, Leicester (0858 880860).

Educational Productions Ltd., Bradford Road, East Ardsley, Wakefield, Yorks. (Wakefield 823971). Also 10 Snow Hill, London EC1 (01 236 6479).

Scripture Union, A. V. A. Dept., PO Box 38, Bristol BS99 7NA.

SPCK, Holy Trinity Church, Marylebone Road, London NW1 (01 387 5282).

The National A.V.A. Centre and Library, Paxton Place, Gipsy Road, London SE27 9SR (01 670 4247).

Various societies and publishers hire and/or sell their own strips, such as CPAS Publications, Fact and Faith Films, The Bible Society, Religious Films and most missionary societies.

Further useful information on A.V.A. can be obtained from the AVA Magazine, a quarterly devoted to audio-visual aids and religious education, obtainable from 17 Nether Street, N. Finchley, London N12.

Overhead projector aids (See also the chapter on this subject)

Bible Map Transparencies (Abingdon) available from Scripture Union or Lion Publishing, Icknield Way, Tring, Herts.

Sheila Pigrem, *Help, I Can't Draw! Vol. 4.* (Kingsway), a pictorial workbook of the Bible.

Staedtler (U.K.) Ltd., Pontyclum, Mid-Glamorgan, CF7 8YJ arrange courses in the use of the OHP.

Vision Screen Services, Riverdale House, North Fambridge, Chelmsford CM3 6NT produce a wide range of audio-visual products including material for the OHP and *Overhead Projection Artwork* by Caroline Stephen.

Visual aid materials and advice

Vision and Venture Ltd., 72, The Street, Kennington, Ashford, Kent TN24 9HS publish a wide range of talks complete with visual aids for purchase. Write for the catalogue.

Maintenance & Equipment News, Dial Publications Ltd., PO Box 249 Ascot, Berks SL5 0BZ regularly include information on AVA, eg Vol.23 No.2 March/April 1981 and Vol.24 No.1 January/February 1982.

Biblical Index

E.T. = Extended Talk (in Part One)

Subject Index

E.T. = Extended Talk (in Part One)

More For All The Family

Edited by Michael Botting

'A marvellous collection of material—I commend the book enthusiastically.'

> From the Foreword by the Bishop of Chester

Following on the success of the earlier volume, *For all the Family*, here are 90 ideas for family service and school assembly speakers, to fit almost any occasion. Clear instructions and diagrams offer outlines for Bible talks that are lively and inexpensive while at the same time drawing on up-to-date audio and video resources.

Editor Michael Botting is well-known for his commitment to reaching families with the Gospel of Jesus. He works for the Diocese of Chester as Joint Director of (Lay) Training.

Kingsway Publications

Help I Can't Draw Vol 4
A Pictorial Workbook of the Bible

by Sheila Pigrem

If you find drawing difficult, then this book is for you!

Most speakers know that visual aids are an important
part of communicating a message, whether it is a talk,
lesson, story or epilogue. This is very different from
actually producing the material, and many teachers,
leaders and ministers are often discouraged by their
efforts with pencil and paper.

Christians should not be satisfied with second best. The
image of the Church is not enhanced by hastily
prepared or scruffy visuals, and those involved in
Christian education and evangelism should use
professional-looking aids.

This book uses simple designs with easy-to-follow,
short-cut methods for reproducing and displaying.
Anyone who follows the helpful hints can produce
quick, effective results which compete with the
standards of the educational and commercial world.

Readers are at liberty to copy, trace over or photocopy
any of the drawings for individual or church use.

Kingsway Publications